# DATE DUE

| | | | |
|---|---|---|---|
| | | | |
| | | | |
| | | | |
| | | | |
| | | | |
| | | | |
| | | | |
| | | | |
| | | | |
| | | | |
| | | | |
| | | | |
| | | | |
| | | | |
| | | | |
| | | | |
| | | | |
| | | | |

12

# THE
# TRIP TO
# BOUNTIFUL

★

**PLAY IN THREE ACTS**

**BY HORTON FOOTE**

★

**DRAMATISTS
PLAY SERVICE
INC.**

## SOUND EFFECTS

The following is a list of sound effects referenced in this play:

Bird call
Bus starting, running, stopping
Accident effect
Traffic noises
Automobile horn

For Lillian Gish
with love and deep gratitude

THE TRIP TO BOUNTIFUL was first produced by The Theatre Guild and Fred Coe on November 3, 1953, at Henry Miller's Theatre, New York City. It was directed by Vincent J. Donehue and the settings were designed by Otis Riggs. The cast was as follows:

MRS. CARRIE WATTS.................................Lillian Gish

LUDIE WATTS......................................Gene Lyons

JESSIE MAE WATTS.................................Jo Van Fleet

THELMA........................................Eva Marie Saint

HOUSTON TICKET MAN................................Will Hare

A TRAVELER......................................Salem Ludwig

SECOND HOUSTON TICKET MAN........................David Clive

HARRISON TICKET MAN..........................Frederick Downs

SHERIFF.........................................Frank Overton

TRAVELERS.........Patricia MacDonald, Neil Laurence, Helen Cordes

## SYNOPSIS OF SCENES

### ACT I
A Houston Apartment

### ACT II
The Trip

### ACT III
A Country Place

# PRODUCTION NOTES

*ACT I.*

The bedroom and living room of a Houston apartment. The walls of these two rooms can be defined by the placement of furniture and by the use of certain necessary fragments of flats needed to contain a door or a window frame.

*ACT II*

The Houston Bus Station, a seat on a Bus, the Harrison Bus Station. The Houston and Harrison Bus stations require no more than a bench each and cut outs to represent ticket windows. Two chairs are all that are required for the Bus seats.

*ACT III*

The house at Bountiful. Since this house is seen through the eyes and heart of Mrs. Watts the actual house can be as symbolic or as realistic as the individual designer chooses. An atmospheric description of this set is included in the text for groups wanting to make use of it.

# THE TRIP TO BOUNTIFUL

## ACT I

### SCENE 1

*The CURTAIN rises. The stage is dark. The lights are slowly brought up and we see the living room and bedroom of a small three room apartment. The two rooms have been furnished on very little money. The living room is R. D. R. In the living room is a sofa that at night has to serve as a bed. It has been made up for the night. U. L. of the room is a door leading out to the hallway, kitchen and bathroom. At the opposite end of this hallway is a door leading to the bedroom. To get back and forth, then, between these two rooms it is necessary to go out into the hallway. C. R., in the living room, is a window looking out on the street. Above the window is a wardrobe in which Mrs. Watts' clothes and other belongings are kept. On top of the wardrobe are a suitcase and Mrs. Watts' purse. A rocking chair is beside the window, and about the room are an easy chair and another straight chair. C., in the living room, is a drop leaf table with two straight chairs at either end. On the table are a small radio and a book. U. C. is a door leading to the outside stairs. Against the rear wall, R., is a desk and on the desk are a phone, a newspaper and a movie magazine.*

*A full moon shines in the window. The two rooms are kept immaculately.*

*The bedroom is smaller than the living room. There is a bed with its headboard against U. S. C. A small table with a bed light stands by the bed. R. C. is a vanity with its back against the imaginary wall separating living room from bedroom. There are two straight chairs in the room, one in front of the vanity. U. L. is a closet with dresses hanging in it.*

*In the living room a woman of sixty is sitting in the rock-
ing chair, rocking back and forth. She is small and thin
and fragile. The woman is Mrs. Watts. She lives in the
apartment with her son, Ludie, and her daughter-in-law,
Jessie Mae.
The lights are out in the bedroom and we can't see much.
Ludie and Jessie Mae are both in bed. Jessie Mae is
asleep and Ludie isn't.
Ludie slips out of his bed, in the bedroom. He starts tip-
toeing out the door that leads to the hallway.
Mrs. Watts continues to rock back and forth in the chair.
She doesn't hear Ludie. She hums a hymn to herself,
"There's not a friend like the lowly Jesus."
Then she hears Ludie.
Ludie is in his early forties. He has on pajamas and a
robe. Ludie has had a difficult life. He had been em-
ployed as an accountant until his health broke down. He
was unable to work for two years. His mother and his
wife are both dependent on him and their small savings
were depleted during his illness. Now he has started working again, but at a very small salary.*

MRS. WATTS. Don't be afraid of makin' noise, Sonny. I'm awake.
LUDIE. Yes, Ma'm. *(He comes into the living room. He comes
over to the window. Mrs. Watts is looking back out the window,
rocking and singing her hymn. He stands behind his mother's
chair looking out the window at moonlight. We can clearly see
his face now. It is a sensitive face. After a moment Mrs. Watts
looks up at Ludie. The rocking ceases for a second.)*
MRS. WATTS. Pretty night.
LUDIE. Sure is.
MRS. WATTS. Couldn't you sleep?
LUDIE. No, Ma'm.
MRS. WATTS. Why couldn't you sleep?
LUDIE. I just couldn't. *(Mrs. Watts turns away from Ludie to
look out the window again. She starts her rocking once more, and
hums her hymn to herself. She is opening and closing her hands
nervously.)* Couldn't you sleep?
MRS. WATTS. No. I haven't been to bed at all. *(Outside the*

8

*window in the street we hear a car's brakes grind to a sudden stop.*)

LUDIE. There's going to be a bad accident at that corner one of these days.

MRS. WATTS. I wouldn't be surprised. I think the whole state of Texas is going to meet its death on the highways. (*Pause.*) I don't see what pleasure they get drivin' these cars as fast as they do. Do you?

LUDIE. No, Ma'm. (*A pause. Mrs. Watts goes back to her humming and her rocking.*) But there's a lot of things I don't understand. Never did and never will, I guess. (*A pause.*)

MRS. WATTS. Is Jessie Mae asleep?

LUDIE. Yes, Ma'm. That's why I thought I'd better come out here. I got to tossin' an' turnin' so I was afraid I was gonna wake up Jessie Mae. (*A pause.*)

MRS. WATTS. You're not worryin' about your job, are you, Sonny?

LUDIE. No, Ma'm. I don't think so. Everybody seems to like me there. I'm thinking about askin' for a raise.

MRS. WATTS. You should, hard as you work.

LUDIE. Why couldn't you sleep, Mama?

MRS. WATTS. Because there's a full moon. (*She rocks back and forth opening and closing her hands.*) I never could sleep when there was a full moon. Even back in Bountiful when I'd been working out in the fields all day, and I'd be so tired I'd think my legs would give out on me, let there be a full moon and I'd just toss the night through. I've given up trying to sleep on nights like this. I just sit and watch out the window and think my thoughts. (*She looks out the window smiling to herself.*) I used to love to look out the window back at Bountiful. Once when you were little and there was a full moon, I woke you up and dressed you and took you for a walk with me. Do you remember?

LUDIE. No, Ma'm.

MRS. WATTS. You don't?

LUDIE. No, Ma'm.

MRS. WATTS. I do. I remember just like it was yesterday. I dressed you and took you outside and there was an old dog howlin' away off somewhere and you got scared an' started cryin' an' I said, "Son, why are you cryin'?" You said someone had told you that when a dog howled a person was dyin' some place. I held you

9

close to me, because you were tremblin' with fear. An' then you asked me to explain to you about dyin', an' I said you were too young to worry about things like that for a long time to come. (*A pause.*) I was just sittin' here thinkin', Sonny. (*She looks up at Ludie. She sees he is lost in his own thoughts.*) A penny for your thoughts.

LUDIE. Ma'm?

MRS. WATTS. A penny for your thoughts.

LUDIE. I didn't have any, Mama. (*She goes back to her rocking.*) I wish we had a yard here. Part of my trouble is that I get no exercise. (*A pause.*) Funny the things you think about when you can't sleep. I was trying to think of the song I used to like to hear you sing back home. I'd always laugh when you'd sing it.

MRS. WATTS. Which song was that, Son?

LUDIE. I don't remember the name. I just remember I'd always laugh when you'd sing it. (*A pause. She thinks a moment.*)

MRS. WATTS. Oh, yes. That old song. (*She thinks for another moment.*) What was the name of it?

LUDIE. I don't know. (*A pause.*)

MRS. WATTS. Less see. Oh, I hate not to be able to think of something. It's on the tip of my tongue. (*A pause. She thinks. She recites the words.*)

> Hush little baby, don't say a word.
> Mama's gonna buy you a mockin' bird.
> And if that mockin' bird don't sing,
> Mama's gonna buy you a diamond ring.

I used to think I was gonna buy you the world back in those days. I remember remarking that to my Papa. He said the world can't be bought. I didn't rightly understand what he meant then. (*She suddenly turns to him, taking his hand.*) Ludie. (*He looks down at her, almost afraid of the question she intends to ask. She sees his fear and decides not to ask it. She lets go of his hand.*) Nothin'. Nothin'. (*A pause.*) Would you like me to get you some hot milk?

LUDIE. Yes, Ma'm. If you don't mind.

MRS. WATTS. I don't mind at all. (*She gets up out of her chair and exits to kitchen. Ludie repeats the lines of the song to himself quietly.*)

LUDIE.

> Hush, little baby, don't say a word.
> Mama's gonna buy you a mockin' bird.

And if that mockin' bird don't sing,
Mama's gonna buy you a diamond ring.
(*Another car comes to a sudden stop out in the street, screeching
its brakes. He peers out the window, his face close against the
screen, trying to see the car. Jessie Mae is awakened by the
screech. She gets out of bed and puts on a dressing gown.*)
JESSIE MAE. (*From the bedroom.*) Ludie! Ludie!
MRS. WATTS. (*Re-enters from hallway.*) You want butter and
pepper and salt in it?
LUDIE. Yes, Ma'm, if it's not too much trouble.
MRS. WATTS. No trouble at all. (*Exits to hallway.*)
JESSIE MAE. (*From the bedroom.*) Ludie.
LUDIE. Come in, Jessie Mae. Mama isn't asleep. (*Jessie Mae goes
out the bedroom into the living room. She immediately turns on
the lights, flooding the room with an ugly glare. Jessie Mae was
probably called very cute when she was young. Now she is hard,
driven, nervous and hysterical.*)
JESSIE MAE. Why don't you turn on the lights? What's the sense
of sitting around in the dark? I don't know what woke me up. I
was sleeping as sound as a log. All of a sudden I woke up and
looked over in bed and you weren't there. Where is your mama?
LUDIE. In the kitchen.
JESSIE MAE. What's she doing out there?
LUDIE. Fixing some hot milk for me.
JESSIE MAE. (*She glances out the hallway.*) Putter, putter, putter.
Honestly! Do you want a cigarette?
LUDIE. No, thanks. (*Jessie Mae takes cigarettes and lighter from
her dressing gown pocket. She struggles with the cigarette lighter.*)
JESSIE MAE. Do you have a match? My lighter is out of fluid. I
have to remember to get some tomorrow. (*Ludie lights her ciga-
rette. A pause. She takes a drag off her cigarette. Ludie gives her
package of matches.*) Thanks. Couldn't you sleep?
LUDIE. Uh. Uh.
JESSIE MAE. How do you expect to work tomorrow if you don't
get your sleep, Ludie?
LUDIE. I'm hopin' the hot milk will make me sleepy. I slept last
night. I don't know what got into me tonight.
JESSIE MAE. You didn't sleep the night before last.
LUDIE. I know. But I slept the night before that.
JESSIE MAE. I don't think your mama has even been to bed.

11

(*Mrs. Watts comes in from hallway with the milk.*) What's the matter with you that you can't sleep, Mother Watts?

MRS. WATTS. It's a full moon, Jessie Mae.

JESSIE MAE. What's that got to do with it?

MRS. WATTS. I never could sleep when there's a full moon.

JESSIE MAE. That's just your imagination. (*Mrs. Watts doesn't answer. She hands Ludie the hot milk. He takes it and blows it to cool it off before drinking. Jessie Mae goes over to a small radio on drop leaf table and turns it on.*) I don't know what's the matter with you all. I never had trouble sleepin' in my life. I guess I have a clear conscience. The only time that I remember having had any trouble sleeping was the night I spent out at Bountiful. The mosquitoes like to have chewed me up. I never saw such mosquitoes. Regular Gallow nippers. (*The radio plays a blues. Jessie Mae picks up a movie magazine from desk and sits in chair by the radio.*) Mother Watts, where did you put that recipe that Rosella gave me on the phone today?

MRS. WATTS. What recipe was that, Jessie Mae?

JESSIE MAE. What recipe was that? She only gave me one. The one I wrote down while I was talkin' to Rosella this mornin'. You remember, I asked you to find me a pencil.

MRS. WATTS. Yes, I remember something about it.

JESSIE MAE. Then I handed it to you and asked you to put it away on the top of my dresser.

MRS. WATTS. Jessie Mae, I don't remember you havin' given me any recipe.

JESSIE MAE. Well, I did.

MRS. WATTS. I certainly have no recollection of it.

JESSIE MAE. You don't?

MRS. WATTS. No, Ma'm.

JESSIE MAE. I swear, Mother Watts, you just don't have any memory at all any more.

MRS. WATTS. Jessie Mae, I think I . . .

JESSIE MAE. I gave it to you this mornin' in this very room and I said to please put it on my dresser and you said I will and went out holding it in your hand.

MRS. WATTS. I did?

JESSIE MAE. Yes, you did.

MRS. WATTS. Did you look on your dresser?

JESSIE MAE. Yes, Ma'm.

MRS. WATTS. And it wasn't there?

JESSIE MAE. No, Ma'm. I looked just before I went to bed.

MRS. WATTS. Oh. Well, let me look around. (*She gets up and goes out the door L., into hallway. Jessie Mae paces around the room.*)

JESSIE MAE. I swear. Have you noticed how forgetful she's getting? I think her memory is definitely going. Honestly, it just gets on my nerves. We're just gonna have to get out a little more, Ludie. No wonder you can't sleep. You get up in the morning, you go to work, you come home, you have your supper, read the paper and then go right off to bed. Every couple I know goes out three or four times a week. I know we couldn't afford it before, so I kept quiet about it. But now you're working again I don't think a picture show once or twice a week would break us. We don't have a car. We don't go to night clubs. We have to do something.

LUDIE. O.K. Why don't we go out one night this week?

JESSIE MAE. I mean, I think we have to. I was talkin' to Rosella about it this morning on the phone and she said she just didn't see how we stood it. Well, I said, Rosella, we have Mother Watts and it's hard for us to leave her alone.

LUDIE. When did you and Rosella get friendly again?

JESSIE MAE. This morning. She just all of a sudden called me up on the telephone. She said she would quit being mad if I would. I said shucks, I wasn't mad in the first place. She was the one that was mad. I told her I was plain spoken and said exactly what I felt and people will just have to take me as I am or leave me alone. I said furthermore, I had told her the truth when I remarked that that beauty parlor must have seen her coming a long way down the road when they charged her good money for that last permanent they gave her. She said she agreed with me now entirely and had stopped patronizing that beauty shop. (*A pause. She goes back to her movie magazine.*) Rosella found out definitely that she can't have any children. . . . (*Mrs. Watts comes into living room at u. L. To Mrs. Watts.*) Walk, don't run. (*Mrs. Watts looks around the room for the recipe. A pause.*) You know your mother's pension check didn't come today. It's the eighteenth. I swear it was due. I just can't understand the Government. Always late. (*Looking up from her reading—then to Mrs. Watts.*) Did you find it?

13

MRS. WATTS. Not yet.

JESSIE MAE. Well, then forget about it. Look for it in the morning.

MRS. WATTS. No, I'm going to look for it until I find it. (*Mrs. Watts goes out of the room* U. L.)

JESSIE MAE. Honestly, Ludie, she's so stubborn. (*She goes back to her movie magazine. Turns the radio dial—radio plays a popular tune.*) I just love this song and this singer: I could just listen to him all day. (*Jessie Mae begins to sing with the singer. There is an immediate knocking upstairs. She continues singing louder than ever. The knocking continues. Finally she jumps up out of her chair. She is very angry.*) Now what are they knocking about? Do you consider this on too loud?

LUDIE. No sense in arguing with them, Jessie Mae.

JESSIE MAE. They'd like it if we didn't breathe.

LUDIE. Well, it is kinda late. (*Ludie turns radio down. Jessie Mae yawns. She goes over to the sofa with the movie magazine.*)

JESSIE MAE. Who played the Captain in "Mutiny on the Bounty"?

LUDIE. Search me.

JESSIE MAE. They're running a contest in here but I never saw such hard questions. (*A pause. She looks up at Ludie.*) Rosella said Jim used to have trouble sleepin'. She said a man told him to lie in bed and count backwards and that would cure him. He tried it and she said it did. She said you start with a hundred and instead of going forward you go backwards. One hundred, ninety-nine, ninety-eight, ninety-seven, ninety-six, ninety-five. . . . She said it would just knock him out.

LUDIE. Jessie Mae, maybe we can take in a baseball game one night this week. The series is getting exciting. I think Houston has the best team they've had in a long time. I'd sure like to be there when they play Shreveport. (*Pause.*) I used to play baseball back at Bountiful. I used to rather play baseball than eat, when I was a kid.

JESSIE MAE. Come on, let's go to bed. (*She gets up. There is another screech of brakes.*) There goes another car smashed up. (*She runs to the window and stands looking out.*) Nope, they missed each other. Six cars smashed up on the Freeway to Galveston I read yesterday in the Chronicle. One right on top of another. One car was trying to pass another car and ran right smack into

14

a third car. Then the ones behind both cars started pilin' up. A lot of them were killed. I bet they were all drunk. Been down to Galveston, gamblin', likely. I think the whole of Houston goes into Galveston gambling and drinking. Everybody but us. I don't see how some people hold down a job the way they drink and gamble. Do you?

LUDIE. No. . . . I don't.

JESSIE MAE. That's why I told Rosella I could hardly keep from callin' up your boss and givin' him a piece of my mind for payin' you the salary he pays you. Like I said to Rosella, you're so steady and so conscientious and they just take advantage of your good nature. Maybe you're too steady, Ludie. (*Ludie has taken a book off the drop leaf table. He goes to the chair, reading it. A pause. Mrs. Watts goes into the bedroom. She turns on the lights in the bedroom and begins a systematic search for the recipe. To Ludie.*) Rosella was glad to hear you're workin' again. She said she was cleanin' out some drawers night before last and had come across some pictures of you and me she'd taken when we started goin' together. I said I don't care to see them. No, thank you. (*Mrs. Watts is looking, now, in Jessie Mae's vanity drawer. She finds the recipe.*) The passin's of time makes me sad. That's why I never want a house with the room to keep a lot of junk in to remind you of things you're better off forgetting. If we ever get any money you wouldn't catch me buying a house. I'd move into a hotel and have me room service. (*Mrs. Watts comes in to living room, holding the recipe.*)

MRS. WATTS. Here's your recipe, Jessie Mae.

JESSIE MAE. Thank you but I told you not to bother. Where did you find it? (*She takes the recipe.*)

MRS. WATTS. In your room.

JESSIE MAE. In my room?

MRS. WATTS. Yes, Ma'm.

JESSIE MAE. Where in my room?

MRS. WATTS. In your dresser drawer. Right hand side.

JESSIE MAE. In my dresser drawer?

MRS. WATTS. Yes, Ma'm. I looked on top of the dresser and it wasn't there an' something said to me . . . (*Jessie Mae rises and angrily throws her package of matches down on table.*)

JESSIE MAE. Mother Watts.

MRS. WATTS. Ma'm.

15

JESSIE MAE. Ludie, how many times have I asked her never to go into my dresser drawer?

MRS. WATTS. I thought you wanted me to find your recipe?

JESSIE MAE. Well, I don't want you to go into my dresser drawers. I'd like a little privacy if you don't mind.

MRS. WATTS. Yes, Ma'm. (*She turns away. She is trying to avoid a fight.*)

JESSIE MAE. (*She is very angry now. She takes Mrs. Watts by the shoulder and shakes her.*) And just let me never catch you looking in them again. For anything. I can't stand people snoopin' in my dresser drawers. (*Mrs. Watts grabs the paper from Jessie Mae and throws it on the floor. She is hurt and angry.*)

MRS. WATTS. All right. Then the next time you find it yourself.

JESSIE MAE. Pick that recipe up, if you please.

MRS. WATTS. Pick it up yourself. I have no intention of picking it up.

JESSIE MAE. (*Shouting.*) You pick that up!

MRS. WATTS. (*Shouting back.*) I won't!

LUDIE. Mama.

JESSIE MAE. (*Shouting even louder.*) You will!

LUDIE. Jessie Mae. For God sakes! You're both acting like children. It's one-thirty in the morning.

JESSIE MAE. You tell her to pick that up.

MRS. WATTS. I won't. (*Mrs. Watts stubbornly goes to her rocking chair and sits.*)

JESSIE MAE. (*Screaming.*) You will! This is my house and you'll do as you're told. (*Ludie walks out of the room. He goes into his bedroom. Jessie Mae crosses to Mrs. Watts.*) Now. I hope you're satisfied. You've got Ludie good and upset. He won't sleep for the rest of the night. What do you want to do? Get him sick again? (*There is a knocking on the floor. Jessie Mae screams up at them.*) Shut up. (*To Mrs. Watts.*) You're going too far with me one of these days, old lady. (*Jessie Mae walks out of the room at U. L. Mrs. Watts is ready to scream back at her, but she controls the impulse. She takes her anger out in rocking violently back and forth. Jessie Mae throws open the door to the bedroom and comes in. Ludie is sitting on the edge of the bed. She marches over to the vanity and sits. She starts to throw things around on top of the vanity. After a moment, Ludie gets up and starts toward her.*)

LUDIE. Jessie Mae.

16

JESSIE MAE. I just can't stand this, Ludie. I'm at the end of my rope. I won't take being insulted by your mother or anyone else. You hear that? (*Ludie rises and stands uncomfortably for a moment. He turns and goes out the bedroom door and into the living room. He stands by the living room door looking at his mother. She stops her rocking. She goes and picks up the recipe. Ludie sees what she is doing and tries to get there first. He is not able to. She hands the recipe to him. He stands there for a moment looking at it. He turns to his mother and speaks with great gentleness.*)
LUDIE. Mama. Will you give this recipe to Jessie Mae?
MRS. WATTS. All right, Ludie. (*She takes the recipe. She starts out of the living room and Ludie stops her. He obviously hates asking the next question.*)
LUDIE. Mama, will you please tell Jessie Mae you're sorry?
MRS. WATTS. Ludie . . .
LUDIE. Please, Mama.
MRS. WATTS. All right, Ludie.
LUDIE. Jessie Mae. (*Mrs. Watts goes out of the room to the bedroom.*)
JESSIE MAE. What do you want, Ludie?
LUDIE. Mama has something to say to you.
JESSIE MAE. What is it? (*Mrs. Watts hands her the recipe.*)
MRS. WATTS. I'm sorry, Jessie Mae, for throwing the recipe on the floor.
JESSIE MAE. I accept your apology. (*Mrs. Watts goes out, reappears in living room. Calling.*) Come on, Ludie. Let's all go to bed.
LUDIE. All right. (*He starts for the living room door u. L.*)
JESSIE MAE. (*Calling.*) And you'd better go to bed, too, Mother Watts. A woman your age ought to have better sense than to sit up half the night.
MRS. WATTS. Yes, Ma'm. Good night, Ludie.
LUDIE. Good night, Mama. (*He waits until his mother sits in the rocking chair and then he turns the lights off in the living room and goes into the bedroom, taking his book with him. Mrs. Watts buries her face in her hands. She is crying. Ludie, now in bedroom.*) Jessie Mae. I know it's hard and all, but for your own sake, I just think sometimes if you'd try to ignore certain things.

17

JESSIE MAE. Ignore? How can you ignore something when it's done right under your very nose?

LUDIE. Look, Jessie Mae.

JESSIE MAE. I know her, Ludie. She does things just to aggravate me. Well, I hope she's happy now. She aggravated me. Now you take her hymn singin'. She never starts until I come into a room. And her poutin'! Why sometimes she goes a whole day just sittin' and starin' out that window. How would you like to spend twenty-four hours a day shut up with a woman that either sang hymns or looked out the window and pouted? You couldn't ignore it and don't tell me you could. No. There's only one thing to do and that's to say quit it, every time she does something like that until she stops for good and all.

LUDIE. I'm not sayin' it's easy, Jessie Mae. I'm only sayin' . . .

JESSIE MAE. Well, let's change the subject. I don't want to get mad all over again. She keeps me so nervous never knowing when I leave whether she is going to try to run off to that old town or not.

LUDIE. Well, she's not going to run off again, Jessie Mae. She promised me she wouldn't.

JESSIE MAE. What she promised and . . .

LUDIE. Now, she can't run off. Her pension check hasn't come. You said yourself. . . . (*Mrs. Watts hears them. She goes to the edge of the rug, lifts it up, and takes the pension check. She stands there for a moment, looking at it, trying to decide whether to take this in to Jessie Mae.*)

JESSIE MAE. Well, I am not too sure that that check hasn't come. Sometimes I think she hides that check and I tell you right now if it is not here tomorrow I am going to search this house from top to bottom.

LUDIE. Well, I know the check will come tomorrow.

JESSIE MAE. I hope so. Rosella says she thinks it's terrible how close I have to stay here. Well, I told Rosella ever since your mother started that running off business I don't feel easy going. I used to love it when I could get up from the breakfast table with an easy mind and go downtown and shop all morning, then get a sandwich and a coke, or a salad at the cafeteria, see a picture show in the afternoon and then come home. That was fun. Shhh. I think I hear your mother still up. (*Mrs. Watts has decided not to give them the check. She is now sitting in her rocking chair,*

18

*rocking and looking out the window. Ludie comes into the living room. She puts the check inside her nightgown.)*
LUDIE. Mama. Are you still up?
MRS. WATTS. Yes I don't feel like sleeping, Ludie. You go on back to bed and don't worry about me.
LUDIE. All right, Mama. *(He goes back to bedroom.)*
JESSIE MAE. Was she still up?
LUDIE. Yes.
JESSIE MAE. I knew it. I never get to go out of the house except for the beauty parlor. I'm not giving that up for anyone. I told Rosella that. I said no one was more faithful to a husband than I was to Ludie, when he was sick, but even then I went out to the beauty parlor once a week. I mean, I had to.
LUDIE. I wanted you to.
JESSIE MAE. I know you did. *(Jessie Mae sings absent-mindedly. She is sitting at the vanity, brushing her hair, putting on face lotion, etc. A pause.)* Next time I see one of those little portable radios on sale, I'm going to get one. It would be nice to have by our bed. It would be so much company for us. *(A pause.)* That was a good supper we had tonight, wasn't it?
LUDIE. Uh. Huh. Mama is a good cook.
JESSIE MAE. Yes. She is. I'll have to hand that to her. And an economical one. Well, she enjoys cooking. I guess you're born to enjoy it. I could never see how anyone could get any pleasure standing over a hot stove, but she seems to. *(A pause.)* Rosella asked me if I realized that it would be 15 years this August since we were married. I hadn't realized it. Had you? *(Ludie thinks for a moment. He counts back over the years.)*
LUDIE. That's right, Jessie Mae. It'll be 15 years this August.
JESSIE MAE. I hate to think of time going that fast. *(A pause.)* I never will forget the night I came home and told Rosella you had proposed. I thought you were the handsomest man alive.
LUDIE. And I thought you were the prettiest girl.
JESSIE MAE. Did you, Ludie? I guess I did have my good features. People used to tell me I looked like a cross between Joan Crawford and Clara Bow. And I thought you were the smartest man in the world. I still do. The thing that burns me up is that you don't let other people know it. Do you remember Sue Carol in the movies?
LUDIE. Sure.

19

JESSIE MAE. I loved her. She was my ideal when I was growing up. She was always so cute in whatever she did. I always tried to act like her, be good company and a sport. (*A pause.*) Sue Carol's married to Alan Ladd now. They've got a bunch of kids. Well, she can afford them. They've got servants and I don't know what all. (*Ludie has his book in his hand. He is walking around the room.*)
LUDIE. Jessie Mae, I've just got to start makin' some more money. I'm thinkin' about askin' for a raise. I'm entitled to it. I've been there six months now. I haven't been late or sick once. I've got to do it. I've got to ask for a raise tomorrow. (*He continues to walk around the room.*) I'm gonna walk into Mr. Douglas' office the first thing in the mornin' and I'm just gonna take the bull by the horns and I'm gonna say, Mr. Douglas, I've got to have a raise starting as of now. We can't live on what you pay us. We have my mother's pension check to help us out and if we didn't have that I don't know what we'd do.
JESSIE MAE. Well, I would.
LUDIE. I don't understand it, Jessie Mae. I try not to be bitter. I try not to. . . . Oh, I don't know. All I know is that a man works eight years with a company. He saves a little money. He gets sick and has to spend two years in bed watching his savings all go. Then start all over again with a new company. (*A pause. He sits on the bed, placing his book on it.*) Of course, the doctor says I shouldn't worry about it. He says I've got to take things like they come. Every day, and that's what I try to do. But how can you help worryin' when you end up every month holding your breath to see if you're gonna make ends meet. (*Jessie Mae gets up from the vanity. She crosses to bed.*)
JESSIE MAE. You can't help being nervous. A lot of people get nervous. (*She sits on the bed and picks up the book.*) What's this book?
LUDIE. It's mine. I bought it at the drug store coming home from the office.
JESSIE MAE. "How to become an Executive." What's that about?
LUDIE. It tells you how to prepare yourself for an executive position. It looks like there might be some helpful things in it. (*Ludie takes the book and leans back against the headboard of the bed, reading. Jessie Mae restlessly looks around the room.*)
JESSIE MAE. You sleepy, Ludie?
LUDIE. No, not yet.

JESSIE MAE. I'm not either. I wish I had something good to eat. I wish the drug store was open. We could get us some ice cream. I wish I had my movie magazine.
LUDIE. Where is it?
JESSIE MAE. In the living room. (*Ludie starts off bed.*)
LUDIE. I'll get it.
JESSIE MAE. No, honey. I don't want to get your mother awake. (*Jessie Mae lies across the foot of the bed. She hums and gets off bed.*) I think I'll get me a cigarette. Want me to get you one?
LUDIE. Thanks. I think I will have one. I can get them.
JESSIE MAE. No. You rest. (*She goes to the vanity and gets a package of cigarettes.*) Rosella cried like her heart would break when she told me she couldn't have children. (*She lights a cigarette and gives one to Ludie.*)
LUDIE. Thanks.
JESSIE MAE. She wanted to know how I stood it not havin' children. I said I don't know about Ludie 'cause you can't always tell what he feels, but I stand it by never thinking about it. (*She walks back to foot of bed and sits.*) I have my own philosophy about those things, anyway. I feel things like that are in the hands of the Lord. Don't you, Ludie?
LUDIE. I guess so.
JESSIE MAE. I've been as good a wife to you as I know how. But if the Lord doesn't want to give us children, all the worryin' in the world won't help. Do you think?
LUDIE. No. It won't.
JESSIE MAE. Anyway, like I told Rosella, I don't have the money to be runnin' around the doctors about it, even if I wanted to. (*A pause.*) Do you have an ash tray?
LUDIE. Right here. (*Ludie gets ash tray from vanity and brings it to her.*) Jessie Mae, if I get a raise the first thing I want you to do is buy yourself a new dress.
JESSIE MAE. Well, thank you, Ludie. (*She goes back to vanity and puts pin curlers in her hair. She puts a hair net on and is finished by end of speech.*) Besides, when you were sick what would I have done if I'd had a bunch of kids to worry me? Your mother said to me the other day, Jessie Mae, I don't know how you and Ludie stand livin' in the city. What are you talkin' about, I said. I didn't start livin' until I moved to the city. Who but a fool would want to live in the country? She wouldn't even listen

21

to my arguments. Honestly, she's so stubborn. I declare, I believe your mother's about the stubbornest woman in forty-eight states. (*She looks at herself in vanity mirror and then gets up laughing.*) Well, I don't look like Joan Crawford now. But who cares? I don't. What are you thinking about?

LUDIE. Oh, I was just thinking about this book. (*A pause. . . . Ludie gets into bed.*)

JESSIE MAE. Ludie, do you ever think back over the past?

LUDIE. No.

JESSIE MAE. I don't either. I started today a little when Rosella brought up that 15 year business. But I think it's morbid. Your mother does that all the time.

LUDIE. I know.

JESSIE MAE. Turn your head the other way. (*He does so. She takes her dressing gown off and slips into bed.*)

LUDIE. My boss likes me. Billie Davison told me today he was positive he did. Billie has been there ten years now, you know. He said he thought he liked my work a lot. (*A pause.*) Feelin' sleepy now?

JESSIE MAE. Uh. Huh. Are you?

LUDIE. Yes, I am. Good night.

JESSIE MAE. Good night. (*Ludie turns off the bed light by the side of the bed. Mrs. Watts is rocking back and forth in her rocker now, working her hands nervously, humming quietly to herself. Ludie hears her and sits up in bed. He gets out of bed and goes into the living room.*)

LUDIE. Mama.

MRS. WATTS. I'm all right, Ludie. I'm just still not sleepy.

LUDIE. You're sure you're feelin' all right?

MRS. WATTS. Yes, I am.

LUDIE. Good night. (*He starts out of the room. She turns to him.*)

MRS. WATTS. Ludie, please, I want to go home.

LUDIE. Mama, you know I can't make a living there. We have to live in Houston.

MRS. WATTS. Ludie, son, I can't stay here any longer. I want to go home.

LUDIE. I beg you not to ask me that again. There's nothing I can do about it. (*Ludie goes back to the bedroom. He gets into bed.*)

JESSIE MAE. Was she still up?

LUDIE. Uh. Huh. Good night.

JESSIE MAE. Good night. (*Mrs. Watts is standing at the back of the rocking chair. She paces around the room thinking what to do. She listens for a moment to see if they are asleep. She decides they are and quietly takes a suitcase down from the top of the wardrobe. She waits a moment then takes some clothing from the drawer of the cupboard and puts them in the suitcase, then she quietly closes it and hides the suitcase under the sofa. She then goes back to her chair, sits and is rocking back and forth violently as the lights fade.*)


# ACT I

## SCENE 2

AT RISE OF CURTAIN, *Mrs. Watts is discovered sleeping in the rocker. Jessie Mae is in bed. Ludie is offstage in the bathroom, washing. Mrs. Watts awakens, looks for check, finds it inside her nightgown and hides it under mattress. She looks out the window to see the time, runs over to Ludie's bedroom to see if he's awake, and runs into the kitchen to put some water on for coffee, calling as she goes.*

MRS. WATTS. Ludie, it's eight-fifteen by the drug store clock. . . .

LUDIE. (*Calling back, offstage.*) Yes'm. (*Mrs. Watts is back in living room with breakfast tray and dishes. Jessie Mae has gotten out of bed and is at the vanity. Ludie sticks his head in living room door.*) Good morning, Mama.

MRS. WATTS. Good morning, son.

LUDIE. Did you get any sleep at all last night?

MRS. WATTS. Yes. Don't worry about me. (*Mrs. Watts goes back into the kitchen, takes the tray out with her. Mrs. Watts comes back with tray and finishes setting table, humming to herself, absent-mindedly. Jessie Mae hollers from next room.*)

23

JESSIE MAE. It's too early for hymn singing. (*Jessie Mae comes into living room.*)

MRS. WATTS. Good morning, Jessie Mae.

JESSIE MAE. Good morning, Mother Watts. (*Mrs. Watts goes out to kitchen. Jessie Mae turns on radio and we hear a popular song. She goes out to bathroom. Ludie enters living room from hallway, puts his jacket on chair, c. Jessie Mae, calling.*) Ludie, turn that radio down, please, before they start knocking again. (*Mrs. Watts enters from the kitchen with coffee, which she sets on table.*)

LUDIE. (*At the radio.*) Would you like me to turn it off?

JESSIE MAE. (*Calling.*) Oh, you might as well.

MRS. WATTS. I'll have your toast ready for you in a minute. (*Crosses into the kitchen. Jessie Mae enters living room from hallway as Mrs. Watts is rushing out.*)

JESSIE MAE. Walk, don't run. I've just got to get me out of this house today, if no more than to ride downtown and back on the bus.

LUDIE. (*Sits at table, drinking coffee.*) Why don't you?

JESSIE MAE. If Mother Watts' pension check comes I'll go to the beauty parlor. I'm just as tense. I think I've got a trip to the beauty parlor comin' to me.

LUDIE. You ought to go if the check comes or not. It doesn't cost that much. (*Mrs. Watts comes in with toast.*)

JESSIE MAE. Mother Watts, will you skip down and see if the mail has come yet? Your pension check ought to be here and I want to get me to that beauty parlor.

MRS. WATTS. Yes, Ma'm. (*Mrs. Watts goes out for the mail at outside door, u. c. Jessie Mae looks after her suspiciously.*)

JESSIE MAE. Ludie, she's actin' silent again. Don't you think she's actin' silent again?

LUDIE. I hadn't noticed. (*He takes a last swig out of his coffee.*)

JESSIE MAE. Well, she definitely is. You can say what you please, but to me it's always a sure sign she's gonna try and run off when she starts actin' silent.

LUDIE. She's not going to run off again, Jessie Mae. She promised me last time she wouldn't. (*He starts up from the table.*)

JESSIE MAE. She just better not. What do you want, Ludie?

LUDIE. I want more coffee.

JESSIE MAE. Well, keep your seat. I'll get it.

24

LUDIE. No, I'll get it.

JESSIE MAE. No. I want to get it. You'll have a tiring day ahead of you. Now rest while you can. (*She goes out to hallway for coffee. Mrs. Watts enters* U. C.)

MRS. WATTS. Where's Jessie Mae?

LUDIE. In the kitchen.

MRS. WATTS. There was no mail, Jessie Mae. (*Jessie Mae comes in* U. L. *with coffee.*)

JESSIE MAE. Had it been delivered yet?

MRS. WATTS. I don't know.

JESSIE MAE. Did you look in the other boxes to see if there was mail?

MRS. WATTS. No, Ma'm. I didn't think to. (*Mrs. Watts goes to the bedroom.*)

LUDIE. I'll look on my way out. Why don't we have an early supper tonight? Six-thirty if that's all right with you and Mama. After supper I'll take you both to the picture show.

JESSIE MAE. That's fine. What would you like to see, Ludie?

LUDIE. Whatever you want to see, Jessie Mae. You know best about picture shows.

JESSIE MAE. Do you want to go downtown or to one of the neighborhood movies? (*She picks up paper from desk.*)

LUDIE. Whatever you want to do, Jessie Mae.

JESSIE MAE. Maybe it would do us good to go downtown. There's something about walkin' into the Majestic or the Metropolitan, or the Loew's State that just picks me up. People dress so much nicer when they're going to see a movie downtown. Of course, on the other hand, I could stand a good double bill myself.

LUDIE. (*Half to himself.*) I want to get to the office a little early this morning. Mr. Douglas is usually in by nine. I'd like a chance to talk to him before the others get there. I think I'm doin' the right thing, askin' for a raise. Don't you?

JESSIE MAE. Sure. I think I'll phone the beauty parlor for an appointment. I hope I can still get one. (*She goes to the phone on desk. Mrs. Watts has been making up the bed. She stops when she hears Jessie Mae dial the phone and goes to the bedroom door to listen.*) Hello, Rita. This is Jessie Mae Watts. Can I have an appointment for my hair? The usual. Uh. Huh. (*She laughs.*) Four o'clock. Nothin' earlier. All right. See you then. (*She hangs up the phone.*) Well, I can't get an appointment until four o'clock.

25

LUDIE. I'm ready to go. Wish me luck on my raise.

JESSIE MAE. Good luck, Ludie. (*He kisses her on the cheek. He calls into the bedroom.*)

LUDIE. Goodbye, Mama.

MRS. WATTS. Goodbye, son. (*Mrs. Watts goes back to making up the bed.*)

LUDIE. Goodbye, Jessie Mae.

JESSIE MAE. So long. Holler if there's any mail down there so we won't be runnin' up and down lookin' for mail that won't be there.

LUDIE. (*Calling back.*) All right. (*Exits outside door, u. c.*)

JESSIE MAE. (*Calling into the bedroom.*) That pension check should have been here yesterday, shouldn't it, Mother Watts?

MRS. WATTS. (*Calling back and trying to seem unconcerned.*) I reckon so.

LUDIE. (*Calling from offstage down stairs.*) No mail for us.

JESSIE MAE. All right! I can't understand about that pension check, can you?

MRS. WATTS. No, Ma'm. (*Jessie Mae casually takes Mrs. Watts' purse off the wardrobe and looks inside. Finding nothing, she closes it and puts it back.*)

JESSIE MAE. I sure hope it isn't lost. You know you're so absent-minded you don't think you put it around the room some place by mistake and forgot all about it. (*Mrs. Watts comes into the living room.*)

MRS. WATTS. I don't believe so. (*Jessie Mae looks around the room. Mrs. Watts watches anxiously everything she does.*)

JESSIE MAE. You know you said you lost that check once before and it took us five days to find it. I came across it under this radio.

MRS. WATTS. I don't think I did that again, Jessie Mae. (*Jessie Mae begins a half hearted search of the room, looking under a vase, a pillow on the sofa, and when she gets to the corner of the rug where the check is hidden, she stoops as if to look under it, but it is only a strand of thread that has caught her attention. She picks it up and goes over to radio, looking under that. Jessie Mae gives up the search and Mrs. Watts goes back to the bedroom. Jessie Mae calls after her.*)

JESSIE MAE. What could I do 'til four o'clock? What are you gonna do today? (*Jessie Mae goes into bedroom.*)

26

MRS. WATTS. Well, I'm going to give the kitchen a good clean-
ing and put fresh paper on the shelves and clean the ice box.
JESSIE MAE. Well, I have a lot of things I have to do. I got some
drawers I can straighten up. Or maybe I'll put some flowers on
that red dress of mine. If I wear the red dress tonight. I really
don't know yet which dress I'm going to wear. Well, if I wear my
red dress tonight, I'll wear this print one to the beauty parlor.
*(She has taken a dress out of her closet and goes out hallway to
the bath room to try it on. Mrs. Watts decides to use this opportu-
nity to run into the living room to get the check. Jessie Mae hears
her running and calls to her from the bath room before she can
reach the rug.)* Mother Watts! *(Mrs. Watts quickly finds something to do in the living room.)*
MRS. WATTS. Yes, Ma'm. *(Jessie Mae comes into the living
room.)*
JESSIE MAE. There you go again. You never walk when you can
run. *(Jessie Mae goes back into the bath room. Mrs. Watts
quickly reaches under the rug and gets the check. She puts it inside
her dress. Then she takes the dishes out to the kitchen. Jessie Mae
continues to lecture her from the bath room.)* You know it's none
of my business, and I know you don't like me to suggest anything,
but I don't think a woman your age should go running around a
three room apartment like a cyclone. It's really not necessary,
Mother Watts. You never walk when you can run. *(Jessie Mae
comes out to the living room with the dress on. She watches Mrs.
Watts.)* I wish for once you'd listen to me.
MRS. WATTS. I'm listening, Jessie Mae.
JESSIE MAE. You're not listening to a word. Mother Watts, are
you feeling all right? You look a little pale.
MRS. WATTS. I'm feeling fine, Jessie Mae. *(Jessie Mae zips up
her dress. Straightens out the skirt and etc. during following
speech.)*
JESSIE MAE. That movie magazine Ludie brought me last night
is running a contest. First prize is a free trip to Hollywood. I'd
like to enter it if I thought I could win. I wouldn't win. I don't
have that kind of luck. I want you to look at the hem of this dress
for me, to see if it's straight.
MRS. WATTS. Yes, Ma'm. *(Mrs. Watts gets a tape measure from
her wardrobe and measures the dress.)*
JESSIE MAE. I'm gonna make Ludie take me to Hollywood one

of these days. I want to visit Hollywood as bad as you want to visit Bountiful.

MRS. WATTS. It measures straight, Jessie Mae. (*She returns tape measure to wardrobe and starts to make her own bed. Jessie Mae walks restlessly around the living room.*)

JESSIE MAE. Do you need anything from the drug store?

MRS. WATTS. Just let me think a moment, Jessie Mae.

JESSIE MAE. Because if you do, I'd walk over to the drug store and have me a fountain coke with lots of chipped ice. We don't need tooth paste. We don't need tooth brushes. I got a bottle of listerine yesterday. Can you think of anything we need from the drug store?

MRS. WATTS. Did you get that nail polish you mentioned?

JESSIE MAE. Oh, yes I have that. I hate to wait around here until four o'clock. I think I'm gonna call Rosella and tell her to meet me at the drug store for a coke. (*She goes to phone and dials. Mrs. Watts is humming to herself as she finishes making up her bed.*) Will you stop that hymn singing? Do you want me to jump right out of my skin? You know what hymns do to my nerves. (*Mrs. Watts stops her humming.*) And don't pout. You know I can't stand pouting.

MRS. WATTS. I didn't mean to pout, Jessie Mae. I only meant to be silent.

JESSIE MAE. (*Hangs up phone.*) Wouldn't you know it. She's not home. I bet she's at the drug store right now. I think I'll go on over to the drug store and just take a chance on Rosella's being there. (*Jessie Mae begins to put her hat on. Mrs. Watts has gotten a hand sweeper from kitchen and is sweeping around the room.*) I can't make up my mind what movie I want to see to-night. Well, I'll ask Rosella. Will you stop that noise for a minute. I'm nervous. (*Mrs. Watts stops sweeping and gets a dust rag from kitchen. She begins to dust the room. Jessie Mae continues putting on her hat and arranging her dress in front of the mirror.*) You know when I first came to Houston, I went to see three picture shows in one day. I went to the Kirby in the morning, and the Metropolitan in the afternoon, and the Majestic that night. People don't go to see picture shows the way they used to. Well, I'm ready. ( *She turns to Mrs. Watts.*) I just want you to promise me one thing. That you won't put a foot out of this house and start that Bountiful business again. You'll kill Ludie if he has to chase

28

all over Houston looking for you. And I'm warning you. The next time you run off I'm calling the police. I don't care what Ludie says. (*Jessie Mae starts out of the room u. c.*) If Rosella calls just tell her I'm at the drug store. (*Mrs. Watts has done her best to continue dusting the furniture during the latter speech, but she has been getting physically weaker and weaker. Finally in a last desperate attempt to keep Jessie Mae from noticing her weakness she grabs hold again of the sweeper trying to support herself. She sways, drops the sweeper and reaches for the sofa to keep from falling, just as Jessie Mae is ready to leave the room.*) Mother Watts . . . (*Jessie Mae runs to her. She is very frightened.*)

MRS. WATTS. (*Trying deperately to control herself.*) I'm all right, Jessie Mae.

JESSIE MAE. Is it your heart?

MRS. WATTS. No. Just a sinkin' spell. Just let me lie down on the sofa for a minute and I'll be all right.

JESSIE MAE. Can I get you some water?

MRS. WATTS. Thank you. (*Jessie Mae runs into kitchen for water.*)

JESSIE MAE. (*Offstage, from kitchen.*) Do you want me to call a doctor?

MRS. WATTS. No, Ma'm.

JESSIE MAE. Do you want me to call Ludie?

MRS. WATTS. No, Ma'm. (*Jessie Mae re-enters living room with a glass of water. Mrs. Watts drinks it.*)

JESSIE MAE. Are you feelin' better?

MRS. WATTS. Yes, I am, Jessie Mae. (*Mrs. Watts gets up off the sofa.*)

JESSIE MAE. Do you think you ought to get up so soon?

MRS. WATTS. Yes, Ma'm. I'm feeling much better already. I'll just sit here in the chair.

JESSIE MAE. All right. I'll sit here for a while and keep you company. (*Mrs. Watts sits in her rocking chair. Jessie Mae sits in her chair, restless as a cat.*) How do you feel now?

MRS. WATTS. Better.

JESSIE MAE. That's good. It always scares the daylights out of me when you get one of those sinkin' spells. Of course, like I told you this morning, you wouldn't be having these sinkin' spells if you'd stop this running around. Well, it's your heart. If you don't want to take care of it no one can make you. But I tell you

29

right now all I need is to have an invalid on my hands. I wish you'd think of Ludie. He's got enough to worry him without your gettin' down flat on your back. (*Phone rings. She goes to it.*) Oh, hello, Rosella. I tried to call you earlier. Oh. You're at the drug store. That's what I just figured. Well, I'd like to, Rosella, but Mother Watts has had a sinking spell again and . . .

MRS. WATTS. You go on, Jessie Mae. I'm gonna be all right. I'll just rest here. There's nothing you can do for me.

JESSIE MAE. Are you sure?

MRS. WATTS. Yes, Jessie Mae. I'm sure.

JESSIE MAE. Well, all right then. Rosella, Mother Watts says she won't need me here. So I think I will come over for a little while. All right. I'll see you in a few minutes. Goodbye. (*She hangs up phone.*) Now you're sure you'll be all right?

MRS. WATTS. Yes, Jessie Mae.

JESSIE MAE. Well, then I'll go on over. Now you call me at the drug store if you need me. You hear?

MRS. WATTS. Yes, Ma'm. (*Jessie May goes out entrance to stairs* U. C. *Mrs. Watts sits for a moment, rocking and using all her will to get her strength back. After a moment she slowly and weakly gets up and goes to the door, listening. She is sure Jessie Mae has gone. She gets her suitcase from under the bed. Then remembers the check, which she takes out, and goes to the desk to endorse it. She takes writing paper and envelope from desk at the same time. While Mrs. Watts is endorsing the check, Jessie Mae comes running back in* U. C. *Mrs. Watts doesn't see her until she has opened the door.*)

JESSIE MAE. I forgot to take any money along with me. (*Jessie Mae is in such a hurry she doesn't see Mrs. Watts. She goes into the bedroom to get her money, which she takes from vanity. Mrs. Watts has just time to get the suitcase and get it back in the wardrobe, stuffs the check inside her dress, and is back to the writing desk when Jessie Mae comes in again.*) Who are you writing to?

MRS. WATTS. I thought I'd drop a line to Callie Davis, Jessie Mae. Let her know I'm still alive.

JESSIE MAE. Why did you decide to do that all of a sudden?

MRS. WATTS. No reason. The notion just struck me.

JESSIE MAE. All right. (*She starts out.*) But just in case you're trying to put something over on me with that pension check, I've told Mr. Reynolds at the grocery store never to cash anything for you. *(She goes out the u. c. door. Mrs. Watts again stands quietly waiting. Then she goes to the door, listening. She decides Jessie Mae has really gone. She gets her hat and coat from wardrobe. She gets her suitcase and goes quietly out the u. c. door as the . . .)*

## CURTAIN FALLS

# ACT II

SCENE: *The lights are bright up on part of a bus terminal in Houston, Texas. It is placed stage Right.* U. C. R. *of this area is a door to the street.* D. R. *is an exit to wash rooms, etc.*

*There is a man sitting on one of the benches eating a sandwich. A pretty blond girl, carrying a suitcase and a magazine, is standing at the ticket window* R. C. *waiting to buy a ticket, a man is standing behind her. The girl's name is Thelma.*

*The Ticket Man is busy on the telephone. He puts the phone down and comes to the front of the window.*

TICKET MAN. Yes?

THELMA. I want a ticket to Old Gulf, please.

TICKET MAN. Yes, Ma'm. *(He reaches for a ticket.)* Here you are. You change busses at Harrison.

THELMA. I know. How much, please?

TICKET MAN. Four eighty.

THELMA. Yessir. *(She gives him the money and steps out of line. Goes to bench and sits, reading a magazine. The Man steps up to the window.)*

MAN. Ticket to Leighton.

TICKET MAN. Leighton. Yes, indeed. *(Mrs. Watts, carrying a suitcase and purse, comes into the terminal from the street entrance* U. C. R. *She is looking all around her to see if Jessie Mae or Ludie have put in an appearance. Satisfied that they haven't, she hurries to the ticket window. She gets in line behind the Man. She is humming the hymn to herself and keeps an eye on the doors all the time. Ticket Man hands the Man his ticket.)* Be seven sixty, please.

MAN. Yessir. *(He gets the money for the Ticket Man. Two People have come up behind Mrs. Watts. The Man gives the Ticket Man the money for the tickets, the Ticket Man reaches for change.)*

32

TICKET MAN. Seven sixty out of ten dollars.
MAN. Thank you. (*He takes his change and exits* D. R. *Mrs. Watts is so busy watching the doors that she doesn't notice it's her turn.*)
TICKET MAN. (*Calling.*) Lady. (*She is still so absorbed in watching, she doesn't hear him.*) Lady. It's your turn. (*Mrs. Watts turns and sees she is next in line. She moves up to the counter.*)
MRS. WATTS. Oh, yes. Excuse me. I'd like a ticket to Bountiful, please.
TICKET MAN. Where?
MRS. WATTS. Bountiful.
TICKET MAN. What's it near?
MRS. WATTS. It's between Harrison and Cotton.
TICKET MAN. Just a minute. (*He takes a book from behind the window on a shelf. He looks inside it. Mrs. Watts is again watching the doors. He looks up.*) Lady.
MRS. WATTS. Oh. Yessir.
TICKET MAN. I can sell you a ticket to Harrison or to Cotton. But there's no Bountiful.
MRS. WATTS. Oh, yes there is, it's between . . .
TICKET MAN. I'm sorry, lady. You say there is, but the book says there isn't. And the book don't lie.
MRS. WATTS. But . . . I . . .
TICKET MAN. (*Impatiently.*) Make up your mind, lady. Cotton or Harrison. There are other people waiting.
MRS. WATTS. Well . . . let me see. . . . How much is a ticket to Harrison?
TICKET MAN. Three fifty . . .
MRS. WATTS. Cotton?
TICKET MAN. Four twenty.
MRS. WATTS. Oh, yes. Well, I'll have the one to Harrison, please.
TICKET MAN. All right. That'll be three fifty, please.
MRS. WATTS. Yessir. (*She reaches for her pocketbook and is about to open it. She turns to the ticket man.*) Can you cash a pension check? You see I decided to come at the last minute and I didn't have time to stop by the grocery store.
TICKET MAN. I'm sorry, lady. I can't cash any checks.
MRS. WATTS. It's perfectly good. It's a government check.

TICKET MAN. I'm sorry. It's against the rules to cash checks.
MRS. WATTS. Oh, is that so? I understand. A rule's a rule. How much was that again?
TICKET MAN. Three fifty.
MRS. WATTS. Oh, yes. Three fifty. Just a minute, sir. I've got it all here in nickels and dimes and quarters. (*She opens her purse and takes a handkerchief out. The money is tied in the handkerchief. She unties it, places it on the counter and begins to count out the amount for the ticket. She counts half aloud as she does it. She shoves a pile of silver towards the Ticket Man.*) Here. I think this is three fifty.
TICKET MAN. Thank you. (*He rakes the money into his hand. She ties her handkerchief back up.*)
MRS. WATTS. That's quite all right. I'm sorry to have taken up so much of your time. (*She picks up her suitcase and starts off.*)
TICKET MAN. Here, lady. Don't forget your ticket. (*She comes running back.*)
MRS. WATTS. Oh, my heavens. Yes. I'd forget my head if it wasn't on my neck. (*She takes the ticket and goes away. The Man next in line steps up to the window. Mrs. Watts goes back to the entrance U. C. R. She peers out and then comes back into the Bus Station. She comes down to the bench. Thelma is seated there, reading. Looks up from her magazine. There is an empty space next to her. Mrs. Watts comes up to it.*) Good evening.
THELMA. Good evening.
MRS. WATTS. Is this seat taken?
THELMA. No, Ma'm.
MRS. WATTS. Are you expectin' anyone?
THELMA. No, Ma'm.
MRS. WATTS. May I sit here then?
THELMA. Yes, Ma'm. (*Mrs. Watts puts the suitcase down along the side of the bench. She looks nervously around the station. All of a sudden she jumps up.*)
MRS. WATTS. Would you watch my suitcase, honey?
THELMA. Yes, Ma'm.
MRS. WATTS. I'll be right back.
THELMA. Yes'm. (*Mrs. Watts goes running back toward the door to the street. Thelma watches her go for a minute and then goes back to reading her magazine. The Man at the ticket window is joined by the Man who is to relieve him for the night. They greet*

34

*each other and the First Ticket Man leaves the bus station. Mrs. Watts comes back to the bench. She sits down and takes a handkerchief out of her purse. She wipes her forehead.)*
MRS. WATTS. Thank you so much.
THELMA. That's all right. *(Mrs. Watts wipes her brow again.)*
MRS. WATTS. Little warm isn't it when you're rushing around?
THELMA. Yes'm.
MRS. WATTS. I had to get myself ready in the biggest kind of hurry.
THELMA. Are you going on a trip?
MRS. WATTS. Yes, I am. I'm trying to get to a town nobody ever heard of around here.
THELMA. What town is that?
MRS. WATTS. Bountiful.
THELMA. Oh.
MRS. WATTS. Did you ever hear of it?
THELMA. No.
MRS. WATTS. You see. Nobody has. Well, it's not much of a town now, I guess. I haven't seen it myself in thirty years. But it used to be quite prosperous. All they have left is a post office and a filling station and a general store. At least they did when I left.
THELMA. Do your people live there?
MRS. WATTS. No. My people are all dead except my son and his wife, Jessie Mae. They live here in the city. I'm hurrying to see Bountiful before I die. I had a sinking spell this morning. I had to climb up on the bed and rest. It was my heart.
THELMA. Do you have a bad heart?
MRS. WATTS. Well, it's not what you call a good one. Doctor says it would last as long as I needed it if I could just cut out worrying. But seems I can't do that lately. *(She looks around the bus station again. She gets up out of her seat.)* Excuse me. Would you keep your eye on that suitcase again?
THELMA. Yes, Ma'm. *(Mrs. Watts hurries back to the* U. C. R. *entrance of the bus station. Thelma picks up her magazine and goes back to reading. Mrs. Watts comes hurrying back to the seat. She doesn't sit down, but stands over by the side.)* Lady. Is there anything wrong?
MRS. WATTS. No, honey. I'm just a little nervous. That's all. *(She hurries back towards the* U. C. R. *door. This time she opens it and goes outside. Thelma goes back to her reading. Mrs. Watts*
35

comes *running back in. She hurries over to the seat and picks up the suitcase. In her confusion, she drops her handkerchief on the floor. Neither she nor Thelma sees it fall.*) Say a prayer for me, honey. Good luck.

THELMA. Good luck to you. (*Mrs. Watts goes running out* D. R. *toward the rest room. Ludie comes in outside door* U. C. *to the bus station. He stands a moment at the entrance, looking all around. He wanders slowly down until he gets to the bench where Thelma is sitting. He pauses here, looking out in front of him and to each side. Jessie Mae comes in* U. C. R. *She is in a rage. She walks over to Ludie.*)

LUDIE. You want to sit down, Jessie Mae?

JESSIE MAE. Yes, I do. If you want to look around, go ahead. I'll wait here.

LUDIE. You looked carefully in the coffee shop?

JESSIE MAE. Yes.

LUDIE. Want me to bring you a coke?

JESSIE MAE. No.

LUDIE. Want me to buy you a movie magazine?

JESSIE MAE. Yes.

LUDIE. All right. I'll be right back. (*He goes back out the outside* U. C. R. *door he came in. Looking around as he goes. Jessie Mae sits down next to Thelma. She takes out a package of cigarettes. She gets her lighter. It doesn't work. She opens her purse and starts looking for a match. She can't find one. She turns to Thelma.*)

JESSIE MAE. Excuse me. Do you have a match? My lighter's out of fluid. (*Thelma reaches in the pocket of her jacket. She finds matches and gives them to her.*) Thank you. (*She lights her cigarette and hands the matches back to Thelma. Jessie Mae takes a deep drag off her cigarette.*) I hope you're lucky enough not to have to fool with any in-laws. I've got a mother-in-law about to drive me crazy. At least twice a year we have to try and keep her from getting on a train to go back to her home town. (*She takes another drag off her cigarette.*) I swear, she always has to spoil everything. My husband was goin' to take us to a double bill to-night at the picture show for the first time in I don't know when. I had called the beauty parlor for an appointment and I couldn't get one till 4 o'clock, see, and I was nervous sitting around the house, and so I went to the drug store for a fountain coke and I come home and what did I find . . . no Mother Watts. So I had

36

to call my husband at the office and say the picture show was off. We've got to go looking for Mother Watts. Oh, she's so stubborn. I could just wring her neck. Her son spoils her that's the whole trouble. She's just rotten spoiled. Do you live with your in-laws?
THELMA. No.
JESSIE MAE. Well, you're lucky. They're all stubborn. My husband is as stubborn as she is. We should be over at the depot right now instead of sitting here. She always tries to go by train, but no. We wait at one railroad station five minutes and the other railroad station for five minutes and because she isn't there, right then, he drags me over here. And don't ask me why she always tries to go by train. That's just how she is. (*She takes another drag off her cigarette. It has gone out.*) Could I trouble you for another match, please? My cigarette has gone out. (*Thelma gets the match for her. Jessie Mae takes it and lights her cigarette.*) Of course, there hasn't been a train to that town in I don't know when. But if you try to tell her that she just looks at you like you're makin' it up. Always before we've been there waitin' for her when she walks into the railroad station, but today I was too trustin'. I gave her all the time in the world to get away. Well, we're payin' for it now. I told Ludie at breakfast she had that silent look, and I bet she tries to run away. But no, he said she wouldn't, because she had promised she wouldn't, and Ludie believes anything she says. I'm just worn out. I've had my fourth Coca-Cola today, just to keep my spirits up. People ask me why I don't have any children. Why? I say I've got Ludie and Mother Watts. That's all the children I need. (*Ludie comes in U. C. R. with a movie magazine. He comes up to Jessie Mae.*) What did you bring me? (*He shows her the magazine.*) Oh, I've seen that one.
LUDIE. (*He puts it absent-mindedly under his arm. He looks around the station.*) Have you seen Mama?
JESSIE MAE. No, you goose. Do you think I'd be sittin' here so calm if I had! Personally, I think we're wastin' our time sittin' here. She always tries to go by train.
LUDIE. But she can't go by train, Jessie Mae.
JESSIE MAE. She doesn't know that.
LUDIE. She's bound to by now. What time did she leave again?
JESSIE MAE. I don't know what time she left. I told you I called from the drug store at 11:30 and she was gone, the sneaky thing.

LUDIE. Well, you see she's had the time to find out a lot of things she hasn't known before. (*Jessie Mae gets up and goes to him.*)

JESSIE MAE. I don't care what you say, Ludie. My hunch is that she's at one of those train stations. We've always found her there. You know how she is. Stubborn. Why, she won't believe them at the depot if they tell her there's not a train to Bountiful. She says there is and you watch, as far as she's concerned that's how it'll have to be. Ludie, I know she's there. I'm never wrong about these things.

LUDIE. All right. Have it your way. Let's go.

JESSIE MAE. Well, now we're here we might as well inquire from someone if they've seen her wanderin' around.

LUDIE. I thought you said she wouldn't come here.

JESSIE MAE. I said I didn't think she would come here. I don't know what the crazy thing will do. I could wring her neck. I can tell you that. I ought to be sitting at the beauty parlor right this very minute.

LUDIE. All right, Jessie Mae. Let's go on back to the depot.

JESSIE MAE. Will you stop rushing me around. I'm so mad I could chew nails. I tell you again I think we ought to just turn this whole thing over to the police. That would scare her once and for all.

LUDIE. Well, we're not going to call any police. We've been through that once and we're . . .

JESSIE MAE. It's for her own good. She's crazy.

LUDIE. (*He is very angry with her.*) Now why do you talk like that? You know Mama isn't crazy. (*A pause.*) I just wish you wouldn't say things like that.

JESSIE MAE. (*Jessie Mae has taken off her hat and hands it to Ludie. She is combing her hair and freshening her make-up during following speech.*) Then why does she keep runnin' off from a perfectly good home like this? To try and get to some old swamp. Don't you call that crazy? I mean, she doesn't have to turn her hand. Hardly. We only have a bedroom and a living room and a kitchen. We're all certainly very light eaters, so cooking three meals a day isn't killing her. And like I told her this morning. She wouldn't be havin' her sinkin' spells if she'd start walkin' like a normal human bein' and not go trottin' all over the place. I said, Mother Watts, please tell me why with a bad heart you insist on

38

running. . . . (*Ludie is getting more and more embarrassed. He sees people looking at them.*)

LUDIE. Well, let's don't stand here arguing. People are looking at us. Do you want to go to the depot or not? (*Jessie Mae turns and sees they're being watched. She lowers her voice but not her intensity.*)

JESSIE MAE. It's your mother. I don't care what you do. Only you better do something. Let me tell you that, or she's gonna clonk out some place. She'll get to Bountiful and die from the excitement and then we'll have all kinds of expenses bringing her body back here. Do you know what a thing like that could cost? Do you realize she had a sinkin' spell this mornin'?

LUDIE. I know. You've told me a hundred times. What can I do about it, Jessie Mae?

JESSIE MAE. I'm trying to tell you what you can do about it. Call the police.

LUDIE. I'm not going to call the police.

JESSIE MAE. Oh, you won't.

LUDIE. No.

JESSIE MAE. Then I think I will. That'll settle it once and for all. (*She goes outside* U. C. R. *Ludie looks around for a minute, then sits down dejectedly in the seat next to Thelma. Thelma has been watching the preceding scene. She has tried not to be seen by them, but the audience should know that she has taken in every single word. Ludie reaches in his back pocket and takes out a handkerchief. He mops his forehead. He notices the magazine under his arm. He takes it in his hand and turns to Thelma.*)

LUDIE. Would you like this? I never read them, and my wife has seen it.

THELMA. Thank you. (*She takes the magazine and puts it in her lap. She goes back to her reading. Ludie looks on the floor and sees the handkerchief that was dropped by Mrs. Watts. He reaches down and picks it up. He recognizes it. He gets up and goes running over to the ticket window.*)

LUDIE. Excuse me. Did an old lady come here and buy a ticket to a town named Bountiful?

MAN. Where?

LUDIE. Bountiful!

MAN. Not since I've been on duty.

LUDIE. How long have you been on duty?

39

MAN. About fifteen minutes.

LUDIE. Where is the man that was on before?

MAN. He's gone home.

LUDIE. Oh. (*He walks away thinking what to do next. He sees Thelma and goes to her.*) Excuse me, Miss.

THELMA. Yes?

LUDIE. I found this handkerchief here that belongs, I think, to my mother. She's run off from home. She has a heart condition and it might be serious for her to be all alone. I don't think she has much money, and I'd like to find her. Do you remember having seen her?

THELMA. Well . . . I . . .

LUDIE. She'd be on her way to a town called Bountiful.

THELMA. Yes, I did see her. She was here talkin' to me. She left all of a sudden.

LUDIE. Thank you so much. (*Jessie Mae has come back in* U. C. R. *Ludie goes up to her.*)

JESSIE MAE. Ludie.

LUDIE. I was right. She was here. The lady there said so.

JESSIE MAE. Well, it's too late now.

LUDIE. But this lady was talking to her.

JESSIE MAE. We're not going to wait. The police and I talked it over. (*Thelma takes advantage of their argument to slip out of the station* U. C.)

LUDIE. (*Turning on Jessie Mae.*) You didn't really call them!

JESSIE MAE. I did, and they said in their opinion she was just trying to get our attention this way and we should just go home and pay her no mind at all.

LUDIE. How can I go home with Mama . . .

JESSIE MAE. The police tell me they have hundreds of case like this every day. They say such things are very common among young people and old people, and they're positive that if we just go home and show her that we don't care if she goes or stays, she'll come home of her own free will.

LUDIE. Jessie Mae . . .

JESSIE MAE. Now, we're going to do what the police tell us to. They say she will come home when she's tired and hungry enough and that makes a lot of sense to me. Now, Ludie, I wish you'd think of me for a change. . . . I'm not going to spend the rest of my life running after your mother.

LUDIE. All right, Jessie Mae. (*He stands there, thinking.*)
JESSIE MAE. Now, come on, let's go. Come on. (*She starts out.*
*Ludie pauses for a moment, thinking. He goes after her.*)
LUDIE. All right. But if Mama is not home in an hour I'm going
after her. . . .
JESSIE MAE. Honestly, Ludie, you're so stubborn. (*They go out*
u. c. r. *as the lights are brought down. Over the loudspeaker we*
*hear the stations being called: Bus leaving for: Newton, Sugarland,*
*Gerard, Harrison, Cotton, Old Gulf, Don Tarle. . . . In the dark-*
*ness we hear the sound of a bus starting, then the noise of the*
*traffic of a downtown city. Brakes grinding, horns honking. This*
*is brought down to almost a whisper. The lights are brought up*
*on the Center section and we see a seat in the bus. Mrs. Watts and*
*Thelma are sitting there. Mrs. Watts is gazing out into the night.*
*Thelma is casually glancing at the movie magazine. After a mo-*
*ment Mrs. Watts turns to her.*)
MRS. WATTS. Isn't it a small world? I didn't know we'd be on
the same bus. Where do you go, honey?
THELMA. Harrison.
MRS. WATTS. Harrison!
THELMA. Yes. I change busses there.
MRS. WATTS. So do I go there. Isn't that nice? It that a moving
picture magazine?
THELMA. Yes, Ma'm. Would you like to look at it?
MRS. WATTS. No, thank you. (*She leans her head back on the*
*seat and turns her head away.*) The bus is nice to ride, isn't it?
THELMA. Yes. It is.
MRS. WATTS. I'm sorry I couldn't take a train, though.
THELMA. I tried to go by train, but you couldn't get connec-
tions tonight.
MRS. WATTS. I know. When I was a girl I used to take excur-
sions from Bountiful to Houston to Galveston. For the day, you
know. Leave at five in the morning and return at ten that night.
The whole town would be down to see you get off the train. I
have such fond memories of those trips. (*A pause. She looks over*
*at Thelma.*) Excuse me for getting personal, but what's a pretty
girl like you doing travelling alone?
THELMA. My husband has just been sent overseas. I'm going to
stay with my family.
MRS. WATTS. Oh, I'm sorry to hear that. Just say the Ninety-

41

first Psalm over and over to yourself. It will be a bower of strength and protection for him. (*She begins to recite with closed eyes.*) "He that dwelleth in the secret place of the most high, shall abide under the shadow of the Almighty. I will say of the Lord, He is my refuge and my fortress: My God; in Him will I trust. Surely He shall deliver thee from the fowler and the noisome pestilence. He shall cover thee with His feathers and under his wing shalt thou trust: His truth shall be thy shield and buckler." (*Thelma covers her face with her hands—she is crying. Mrs. Watts looks up and sees her.*) Oh, I'm sorry. I'm sorry, honey.

THELMA. That's all right. I'm just lonesome for him.

MRS. WATTS. Keep him under the Lord's wing, honey, and he'll be safe.

THELMA. Yes, Ma'm. (*She dries her eyes.*) I'm sorry. I don't know what gets into me.

MRS. WATTS. Nobody needs be ashamed of crying. I guess we've all dampened our pillows sometime or other. I have, goodness knows.

THELMA. If I could only learn not to worry.

MRS. WATTS. I know. I guess we all ask that. Jessie Mae, my daughter-in-law, don't worry. What for? She says. Well, like I tell her that's a fine attitude if you can cultivate it. Trouble is I can't any longer.

THELMA. It is hard.

MRS. WATTS. I didn't use to worry. I was so carefree as a girl. Had lots to worry me, too. Everybody was so poor back in Bountiful. But we got along. I said to Papa once after our third crop failure in a row, whoever gave this place the name of Bountiful? His Papa did, he said, because in those days it was a land of plenty. You just had to drop seeds in the ground and the crops would spring up. Cotton and corn and sugar cane. I still think it's the prettiest place I know of. Jessie Mae says it's the ugliest. But she just says that I know to make me mad. She only saw it once, and then on a rainy day, at that. She says it's nothing but a swamp. That may be, I said, but it's a mighty pretty swamp to me. And then Sonny, that's my boy, Ludie, I call him Sonny, he said not to answer her back. He said it only caused arguments. And nobody ever won an argument with Jessie Mae, and I guess that's right. (*A pause. She looks out into space.*)

THELMA. Mrs. Watts . . .

MRS. WATTS. Yes?

THELMA. I think I ought to tell you this . . . I . . . I don't want you to think I'm interfering in your business . . . but . . . well . . . you see your son and your daughter-in-law came in just after you left. . . .

MRS. WATTS. I know. I saw them coming. That's why I left so fast.

THELMA. Your son seemed very concerned.

MRS. WATTS. Bless his heart.

THELMA. He found a handkerchief that you had dropped.

MRS. WATTS. Oh, mercy. That's right, I did.

THELMA. He asked me if I had seen you. I felt I had to say yes. I wouldn't have said anything if he hadn't asked me.

MRS. WATTS. Oh, that's all right. I would have done the same thing in your place. Did you talk to Jessie Mae?

THELMA. Yes.

MRS. WATTS. Isn't she a sight? I bet she told you I was crazy. . . .

THELMA. Well . . .

MRS. WATTS. Oh, don't be afraid of hurting my feelings. Poor Jessie Mae, she thinks everybody's crazy that don't want to sit in the beauty parlor all day and drink Coca-colas. She tells me a million times a day I'm crazy. That's the only time Ludie will talk back to her. He gets real mad when she calls me crazy. I think Ludie knows how I feel about getting back to Bountiful. Once when I was talkin' about somethin' we did back there in the old days, he just broke out cryin'. He was so overcome he had to leave the room. (*A pause. Mrs. Watts starts to hum . . . "There's Not a Friend Like the Lowly Jesus."*)

THELMA. That's a pretty hymn. What's the name of it?

MRS. WATTS. "There's Not a Friend Like the Lowly Jesus." Do you like hymns?

THELMA. Yes, I do.

MRS. WATTS. So do I. Jessie Mae says they've gone out of style . . . but I don't agree. I always sing one walking down the street or riding in the streetcar. Keeps my spirits up. What's your favorite hymn?

THELMA. Oh, I don't know.

MRS. WATTS. The one I was singin' is mine. I bet I sing it a hundred times a day. When Jessie Mae isn't home. Hymns make

Jessie Mae nervous. (*A pause.*) Did Ludie mention my heart condition?

THELMA. Yes, he did.

MRS. WATTS. Poor Ludie. He worries about it so. I hated to leave him. Well, I hope he'll forgive me in time. So many people are nervous today. He wasn't nervous back in Bountiful. Neither was I. The breeze from the Gulf would always quiet your nerves. You could sit on your front gallery and smell the ocean blowing in around you. (*A pause.*) I regret the day I left. But I thought it was the best thing at the time. There were only three families left there then. Farming was so hard to make a living by, and I had to see to our farm myself; our house was old and there was no money to fix it with, nor send Ludie to school. So I sold off the land and gave him an education. Callie said I could always come back and visit her. She meant it, too. That's who I'm going to stay with now. Callie Davis. I get a card from her every Christmas. I wrote her last week and told her to expect me. Told her not to answer though on account of Jessie Mae opens all my mail. I didn't want her to know I was going. She'd try to stop me. Jessie Mae hates me. I don't know why, but she hates me. (*A pause.*) Hate me or not. I gotta get back and smell that salt air and work that dirt. I'm gonna spend the whole first month of my visit workin' in Callie's garden. I haven't had my hands in dirt in twenty years. My hands feel the need of dirt. (*A pause.*) Do you like to work the ground?

THELMA. I never have.

MRS. WATTS. Try it sometimes. It'll do wonders for you. I bet I'll live to be a hundred once I can get outside again. It was being cooped up in those two rooms that was killing me. I used to work the land like a man. Had to when Papa died. . . . I got two little babies buried there. Renee Sue and Douglas. Diphtheria got Renee Sue. I never knew what carried Douglas away. He was just weak from the start. I know Callie's kept their graves weeded. Oh, if my heart just holds out until I get there. (*A pause.*) Where do you go from Harrison?

THELMA. Old Gulf. My family have just moved there from Louisiana. I'll stay there with them until my husband comes home again.

MRS. WATTS. That's nice.

THELMA. It'll be funny living at home again.

44

MRS. WATTS. How long have you been married?

THELMA. A year. My husband was anxious for me to go. He said he'd worry about my being alone. I'm the only child and my parents and I are very close.

MRS. WATTS. That's nice.

THELMA. My father being in the oil business we've always moved around a lot. I guess I went to school in fifteen different towns along the Coast. I guess moving around like that made me and my mother and father even closer. I hoped so my mother and daddy would like my husband and he'd like them. I needn't have worried. They hit it off from the very first. Mother and daddy say they feel like they have two children now. A son and a daughter.

MRS. WATTS. Isn't that nice? I've heard people say that when your son marries you lose a son, but when your daughter marries you get a son. (*A pause.*) What's your husband's name?

THELMA. Robert.

MRS. WATTS. That's a nice name.

THELMA. I think so. But I guess any name he had I would think was nice. I love my husband very much. Lots of girls I know think I'm silly about him, but I can't help it. (*A pause.*)

MRS. WATTS. I wasn't in love with my husband. (*A pause.*) Do you believe we are punished for what we do wrong? I sometimes think that's why I've had all my trouble. I've talked to many a preacher about it, all but one said they didn't think so. But I can't see any other reason. Of course, I didn't lie to my husband. I told him I didn't love him, that I admired him, which I did, but I didn't love him. That I'd never love anybody but Ray John Murray as long as I lived and I didn't, and I couldn't help it. Even after my husband died and I had to move back with Mama and Papa I used to sit on the front gallery every morning and every evening just to nod hello to Ray John Murray as he went by the house to work at the store. He went a block out of his way to pass the house. He never loved nobody but me.

THELMA. Why didn't you marry him?

MRS. WATTS. His papa and my papa didn't speak. My papa forced me to write a letter saying I never wanted to see him again and he got drunk and married out of spite. I felt sorry for his wife. She knew he never loved her. (*A pause.*) I don't think about those things any more. But they're all part of Bountiful and I guess

45

that's why I'm starting to think of them again. You're lucky to be married to the man you love, honey.

THELMA. I know I am.

MRS. WATTS. Awfully lucky. (*A pause. She looks out the window.*) Did you see that star fall over there?

THELMA. No.

MRS. WATTS. It was the prettiest thing I ever saw. You can make a wish on a falling star, honey.

THELMA. I know. It's too bad I didn't see it.

MRS. WATTS. You take my wish.

THELMA. Oh, no.

MRS. WATTS. Go on. I've gotten mine already. I'm on my way to Bountiful.

THELMA. Thank you. (*A pause. Thelma closes her eyes. Mrs. Watts watches her for a moment.*)

MRS. WATTS. Did you make your wish?

THELMA. Yes, I did. (*Mrs. Watts leans her head back on the seat. She hums to herself. Thelma leans her head back, too. They close their eyes. The lights fade. The lights on the area L. are brought up. It is the Harrison Bus Station. An Old Man is inside the ticket window, c. L. with his head on the ledge asleep. He wakes up. He comes out of the cage into the room, yawning and stretching. We hear a bus pull up in the distance and stop. He starts for the entrance of the Bus Station, u. c. L., as Thelma comes in carrying her suitcase and Mrs. Watts' suitcase.*)

TICKET MAN. Want any help with those bags?

THELMA. No, thank you. (*The Ticket Man turns a light on in the Station. Thelma takes the bags and puts them down beside a bench. She goes over to the Ticket Man.*) Excuse me.

TICKET MAN. Yes?

THELMA. Is the bus to Old Gulf going to be on time?

TICKET MAN. Always is.

THELMA. Thank you. (*Thelma goes back to her seat near the suitcases. Mrs. Watts comes in u. L. c. She sees the Ticket Man. She speaks to him.*)

MRS. WATTS. Good evening. (*To Thelma.*) What time is it, honey?

THELMA. Twelve o'clock.

MRS. WATTS. Twelve o'clock. I bet Callie will be surprised to see me walk in at twelve o'clock.

THELMA. Did you tell her you were coming today?
MRS. WATTS. No. I couldn't. Because I didn't know. I had to
wait until Jessie Mae went to the drug store.
TI IELMA. My bus is leaving in half an hour.
MRS. WATTS. Oh, I see. I guess I'd better be finding out how
I'm going to get on out to Bountiful.
THELMA. You sit down. I'll find the man.
MRS. WATTS. Thank you. (*She sits on the bench. Thelma goes
over to the Ticket Man at the door. He is busy bringing in morn-
ing papers left by the bus.*)
THELMA. Excuse me again.
TICKET MAN. Yes?
THELMA. My friend here wants to know how she can get to
Bountiful.
TICKET MAN. Bountiful?
THFI MA Yes
TICKET MAN. What's she going there for? (*Mrs. Watts comes
up to the Ticket Man.*)
MRS. WATTS. I'm going to visit my girlhood friend.
TICKET MAN. I don't know who that's gonna be. The last person
in Bountiful was Mrs. Callie Davis. She died day before yester-
day. That is they found her day before yesterday. She lived all
alone so they don't know exactly when she died.
MRS. WATTS. Callie Davis!
TICKET MAN. Yes, Ma'm. They had the funeral this morning
Was she the one you were going to visit?
MRS. WATTS. Yessir. She was the one. She was my friend. My
girlhood friend. (*Mrs. Watts stands for a moment. Then she goes
to the bench. She seems very old and tired and defeated. Thelma
crosses to Ticket Man.*)
THELMA. Is there a hotel here?
TICKET MAN. Yes'm. The Riverview.
THELMA. How far is it?
TICKET MAN. About five blocks.
THELMA. Is there a taxi around?
TICKET MAN. No, Ma'm. Not this time of night.
TI IELMA. Thank you. (*The Man goes back into the ticket win
dow. Thelma goes over to Mrs. Watts at the bench. She speaks
to her with great sympathy.*) What'll you do now, Mrs. Watts?

MRS. WATTS. I'm thinking, honey. I'm thinking. It's come as quite a blow.

THELMA. I'm sorry. I'm so sorry.

MRS. WATTS. I know. I know. (*A pause. Her strength and her will reviving.*) It's come to me what to do. I'll go on. That much has come to me. To go on. I feel my strength and my purpose strong within me. I'll go on to Bountiful. I'll walk those twelve miles if I have to. (*She is standing now.*)

THELMA. But if there's no one out there what'll you do this time of night? (*Thelma gets her to sit back down.*)

MRS. WATTS. Oh, yes. I guess that's right.

THELMA. I think you should wait until morning.

MRS. WATTS. Yes. I guess I should. Then I can hire someone to drive me out. You know what I'll do. I'll stay at my own house, or what's left of it. Put me in a garden. I'll get along fine with the help of my government checks.

THELMA. Mrs. Watts, the man says there's a hotel not too far away. I think you'd better let me take you there.

MRS. WATTS. Oh, no thank you. I wouldn't want to waste my money on a hotel. They're high as cats' backs you know. I'll just sleep right here on this bench. Put my coat under my head, hold my purse under my arm. (*She puts the coat down on the bench like a pillow. She begins to look around for her purse. She has lost it.*) My purse! (*She begins to search frantically.*) Have you seen my purse, honey?

THELMA. Why, no. (*They begin to look around for it.*)

MRS. WATTS. Oh, good heavens. I remember now. I left my purse on the bus. (*Thelma runs to the entrance and looks out.*)

THELMA. You're sure you left it there?

MRS. WATTS. (*Joining her.*) Yes. I am. I remember now. I didn't have it when I got off that bus. I kept thinking something was missing, but then I decided it was my suitcase that you had brought in for me. What am I gonna do, honey? All I have in the world is in that purse. (*Thelma and Mrs. Watts go back to the ticket window. The Man is drowsing.*)

THELMA. Excuse me again.

TICKET MAN. Yeah?

THELMA. This lady left her purse on the bus.

TICKET MAN. All right. I'll call ahead. How can you identify it?

MRS. WATTS. It's a plain brown purse.

48

TICKET MAN. How much money?

MRS. WATTS. Thirty-five cents and a pension check.

TICKET MAN. Who was the check made out to?

MRS. WATTS. To me. Mrs. Carrie Watts.

TICKET MAN. All right. I'll call up about it.

MRS. WATTS. Oh, thank you. You're most kind.

THELMA. How long will it take to get it back?

TICKET MAN. Depends. If I can get ahead of the bus at Don Tarle, I can get them to send it back on the Victoria Bus and it should be here in a couple of hours.

MRS. WATTS. That's awful kind of you. *(He goes. Thelma and Mrs. Watts go back to the bench.)* I don't know what I would have done without you.

THELMA. Try not to worry about the purse.

MRS. WATTS. I won't. *(They sit on the bench.)* I'm too tired to worry. Be time enough to start worrying when I wake up in the morning.

THELMA. Why don't you go on to sleep now if you can?

MRS. WATTS. Oh, I thought I'd stay up and see you off.

THELMA. No. You go on to sleep.

MRS. WATTS. I couldn't go right off to sleep now. I'm too wound up. You know I don't go on a trip every day of my life. *(The Ticket Man comes over to them on the bench.)*

TICKET MAN. You're lucky. Bus hadn't gotten to Don Tarle yet. If they can find the purse it'll be here around five.

MRS. WATTS. Thank you. Thank you so much.

THELMA. Make you feel better?

MRS. WATTS. Yes. It does. Of course, everything has seemed to work out today. Why is it some days everything works out, and some days nothing works out. What I mean, is, I've been trying to get on that bus for Bountiful for over five years. Usually Jessie Mae and Ludie find me before I ever get inside the railroad station good. Today, I got inside both the railroad station and the bus station. Bought a ticket, seen Ludie and Jessie Mae before they saw me. Hid out. Met a pretty friend like you. Lost my purse, and now I'm having it found for me. I guess the good Lord is just with me today. *(A pause.)* I wonder why the Lord isn't with us every day? It would be so nice if He was. Well, maybe then we wouldn't appreciate so much the days when He's on our side. Or maybe He's always on our side and we don't know it. Maybe

49

I had to wait twenty years cooped up in a city before I could appreciate getting back here. (*A pause. Thelma rests her head back on the bench. Mrs. Watts rests her head. She hums her hymn.*) It's so nice being able to sing a hymn when you want to. I'm a happy woman, young lady. A very happy woman.

THELMA. I still have a sandwich left. Will you have one?

MRS. WATTS. Sure you don't want it?

THELMA. No. I'm full.

MRS. WATTS. Then I'll have a half, thank you. (*Thelma gets the sandwich from her suitcase and unwraps it.*)

THELMA. Take the whole sandwich. I'm not hungry.

MRS. WATTS. No, thank you. Just half. You know I don't eat much. Particularly if I'm excited. (*She rises and stands nibbling on the sandwich and walking around the room.*) You know, I came to my first dance in this town.

THELMA. Did you?

MRS. WATTS. Yes, Ma'm. It was the summertime. My father couldn't decide if he thought dancin' was right or not. But my mother said she had danced when she was a girl and I was gonna dance. And so I went. The girls from all over the county came for this dance. It was at the Opera House. I forget what the occasion was. Somethin' special though. (*A pause. She looks at Thelma. She goes over to her.*) Do you know something, young lady? If my daughter had lived I would have wanted her to be just like you.

THELMA. Oh, thank you.

MRS. WATTS. (*With great tenderness.*) Just like you. Sweet and considerate and thoughtful.

THELMA. Oh, no . . . I'm . . .

MRS. WATTS. Oh, yes. Sweet and considerate and thoughtful. And pretty.

THELMA. Well, thank you. (*A pause.*) Mrs. Watts . . . I hope you don't mind my askin' this, but I worry about your son. Are you going to let him know where you are?

MRS. WATTS. Oh, yes, Ma'm. As soon as I get that check cashed I'm going to send him a telegram. (*The Ticket Man comes by checking his watch as he passes. Mrs. Watts follows after him.*) I was tellin' my little friend here that I came to my first dance in this town.

TICKET MAN. Is that so?

MRS. WATTS. Yes. And I've been to Harrison quite a few times in my life, shopping.

TICKET MAN. (*To Thelma.*) You'd better get outside, Miss. Bus will be up the road. It won't wait this time of night unless it sees we have a passenger.

THELMA. All right. (*She gets her suitcase.*) Goodbye, Mrs. Watts.

MRS. WATTS. (*Following her to the door.*) Goodbye, honey. Good luck to you. And thank you for everything.

THELMA. That's all right. Good luck to you.

MRS. WATTS. Thank you. (*Thelma kisses her. Thelma goes out into the night, followed by the Ticket Man. Mrs. Watts stands at the door watching Thelma. We hear a bus pulling up. Mrs. Watts waves. We hear the bus leave. The Ticket Man comes back inside the Bus Station.*)

TICKET MAN. Are you gonna stay here all night?

MRS. WATTS. I have to. Everything I have is in that purse and we can't go any place without money.

TICKET MAN. I guess that's right. (*He starts away.*)

MRS. WATTS. Do they still have dances in Borden's Opera House?

TICKET MAN. No, Ma'm. It's torn down. They condemned it, you know. (*He starts on. He pauses.*) Did you ever know anybody in Harrison?

MRS. WATTS. I knew a few people when I was a girl. Priscilla Nytelle. Did you know her?

TICKET MAN. No, Ma'm.

MRS. WATTS. Nancy Lee Goodhue?

TICKET MAN. No, Ma'm.

MRS. WATTS. The Fay girls?

TICKET MAN. No, Ma'm.

MRS. WATTS. I used to trade in Mr. Ewing's store. I knew him to speak to.

TICKET MAN. Which Ewing was that?

MRS. WATTS. George White Ewing.

TICKET MAN. He's dead.

MRS. WATTS. Is that so?

TICKET MAN. Been dead for twelve years.

MRS. WATTS. Is that so?

TICKET MAN. He left quite a bit of money, but his son took over his store and lost it all. Drank.

MRS. WATTS. Is that so? One thing I can say about my boy is that he never gave me any worry that way.

TICKET MAN. Well, that's good. I've got one boy that drinks and one boy that doesn't. I can't understand it. I raised them the same way.

MRS. WATTS. I know. I've known of other cases like that. One drinks. The other doesn't.

TICKET MAN. A friend of mine has a girl that drinks. I think that's the saddest thing in the world.

MRS. WATTS. Isn't it? (*A pause.*)

TICKET MAN. Well. Goodnight.

MRS. WATTS. Goodnight. (*Ticket Man stands waiting to switch off the light while Mrs. Watts takes her suitcase and coat and makes a bed for herself on the bench. She lies down. He goes inside the ticket booth. He sticks his head out the cage.*)

TICKET MAN. Goodnight.

MRS. WATTS. Goodnight. (*He turns the light inside the ticket window out. Mrs. Watts is humming quietly to herself. Her humming fades away as the lights are faded out. The lights are brought up. The Ticket Man is in his office sound asleep and snoring slightly. The door opens and a Man comes in. He is the Sheriff. He stands by the door for a moment looking around the Bus Station. He sees Mrs. Watts lying on the bench asleep. He goes over to her and looks down. He stands for a moment watching her sleep. He looks over at the ticket window and sees the Man is asleep. The Sheriff goes over to the Ticket Man. He shakes him.*)

SHERIFF. Come on, Roy, wake up.

TICKET MAN. Yeah? (*He opens his eyes. He sees the Sheriff. He comes out to the Sheriff.*) Oh, hello, Sheriff.

SHERIFF. How long has that old woman been here?

TICKET MAN. About four hours.

SHERIFF. Did she get off the bus from Houston?

TICKET MAN. Yessir. I know her name. It's Watts. She left her purse on the bus and I had to call up to Don Tarle about it.

SHERIFF. Have you got her purse?

TICKET MAN. Yes. It just came.

SHERIFF. She's the one, all right. I've had a call from the Houston Police to hold her until her son can come for her.

52

TICKET MAN. She said she used to live in Bountiful.

SHERIFF. Yeah. I believe I remember some Watts' a long time ago over that way. I think that old ramshackly house about to fall into the Brazos River belonged to them.

TICKET MAN. That right? They must have been before my time. She asked me about a lot of people I never heard of. She claimed she was going to visit Miss Callie Davis. I told her she was dead. What do the police want her for?

SHERIFF. Police don't. It's her son. He wants to take her back home. Claims she's not responsible. Did she act crazy to you?

TICKET MAN. Not that I noticed. Is she crazy?

SHERIFF. They say so. Harmless, but hipped on running away from Houston to get back here. (*He starts over to her to wake her up. He stands looking at her for a moment. He comes back to the Ticket Man.*) Poor old thing. She's sleeping so sound. I don't have the heart to wake her up. I'll tell you what, I'll go down and call Houston . . . tell them she's here. Her son is coming in his car. He should be here around seven-thirty. I'll be back in ten minutes. If she gives you any trouble just call me. Keep your eye on her.

TICKET MAN. All right. (*The Sheriff goes out and the Ticket Man follows him. Comes back in carrying a crate. He bumps it accidentally against the door. This wakes Mrs. Watts up. She opens her eyes. She looks around trying to remember where she is. Then she sees the Ticket Man.*)

MRS. WATTS. Good morning.

TICKET MAN. Good morning.

MRS. WATTS. Could you tell me the time?

TICKET MAN. It's around four thirty.

MRS. WATTS. Thank you. Did my purse arrive?

TICKET MAN. Yes, Ma'm. (*He reaches under the ticket window to a ledge and gets the purse for her. He hands the purse to her.*)

MRS. WATTS. Thank you so much. I wonder if you could cash a check for me?

TICKET MAN. I'm sorry. I can't.

MRS. WATTS. It's a government check and I have identification.

TICKET MAN. I'm sorry. I can't.

MRS. WATTS. Do ·you know where I could get a check cashed?

TICKET MAN. Why? (*She starts to gather up her coat and suitcase.*)

53

MRS. WATTS. I need money to get me started in Bountiful. I want to hire someone to drive me out there and look at my house and get a few groceries. Try to find a cot to sleep on. (*She has the coat and suitcase.*)

TICKET MAN. I'm sorry, lady. You're not going to Bountiful.

MRS. WATTS. Oh, yes, I am. You see . . .

TICKET MAN. I'm sorry, lady. You're not going any place right now. I have to hold you here for the Sheriff.

MRS. WATTS. The Sheriff?

TICKET MAN. Yes, Ma'm. (*A pause.*)

MRS. WATTS. You're joking with me!? Don't joke with me. I've come too far.

TICKET MAN. I'm sorry. That's how it is.

MRS. WATTS. What has the Sheriff got to do with me?

TICKET MAN. He came a few minutes ago while you were asleep and said I was to keep you here until your son arrived in his car this morning.

MRS. WATTS. My son hasn't got a car, so I don't believe you. I don't believe you.

TICKET MAN. It's the truth. He'll be here in a little while, and you can ask him yourself. (*A pause.*)

MRS. WATTS. Then you're not joking?

TICKET MAN. No. (*She takes her coat and suitcase and runs for the entrance. He senses what she is going to do and gets there first—blocking her way.*)

MRS. WATTS. All right. But I'm going, do you understand? You'll see. This is a free country. And I'll tell him that. No Sheriff or king or president will keep me from going back to Bountiful.

TICKET MAN. All right. You tell him that. (*She comes back into the room. She is desperate.*)

MRS. WATTS. What time is my son expected?

TICKET MAN. Sheriff says around seven-thirty.

MRS. WATTS. What time is it now?

TICKET MAN. I told you around four-thirty.

MRS. WATTS. Where can I get me a driver?

TICKET MAN. Ma'm?

MRS. WATTS. If you can get me a driver, I can make it to Bountiful and back way before seven-thirty. . . .

TICKET MAN. Look, lady . . .

MRS. WATTS. That's all I want. That's all I ask. Just to see it.

54

To stand on the porch of my own house, once more. Walk under the trees. I swear, I would come back then meek as a lamb. . . .

TICKET MAN. Lady . . .

MRS. WATTS. Last night, I thought I had to stay. I thought I'd die if I couldn't stay. But I'll settle for less now. Much, much less. An hour. A half hour. Fifteen minutes.

TICKET MAN. Lady, it ain't up to me. I told you the Sheriff.

MRS. WATTS. (Screaming.) Then get me the Sheriff.

TICKET MAN. Look, lady . . .

MRS. WATTS. Get me the Sheriff. The time is going. They'll have me locked in those two rooms again soon. The time is going . . . the time is . . . (The Sheriff comes in. The Sheriff goes over to Mrs. Watts.)

SHERIFF. Mrs. Watts?

MRS. WATTS. Yessir. (She looks up at him. She puts the coat and suitcase down.) Are you the Sheriff?

SHERIFF. Yes, Ma'm.

MRS. WATTS. I understand my son will be here at seven-thirty to take me back to Houston.

SHERIFF. Yes, Ma'm.

MRS. WATTS. Then listen to me, sir. I've waited a long time. Just to get to Bountiful. Twenty years I've been walkin' the streets of the city, lost and grieving. And as I've grown older and my time approaches, I've made one promise to myself, to see my home again . . . before I die . . .

SHERIFF. Lady . . . I . . .

MRS. WATTS. I'm not asking that I not go back. I'm willing to go back. Only let me travel these twelve miles first. I have money. I can pay . . .

SHERIFF. I think that's between you and your son.

MRS. WATTS. Ludie? Why, he's got to do whatever Jessie Mae tells him to. I know why she wants me back. It's for my government check.

SHERIFF. I don't know anything about that. That's between you and your son.

MRS. WATTS. Won't you let me go?

SHERIFF. No. Not unless your son takes you.

MRS. WATTS. All right. Then I've lost. I've come all this way only to lose. (A pause. She stands behind the bench supporting herself. She seems very tired and defeated. She speaks very quietly

55

*and almost to herself.*) I've kept thinking back there day and night in those two rooms, I kept thinkin' . . . and it may mean nothin' at all to you, but I kept thinkin' . . . that if I could just set foot there for a minute . . . even . . . a second . . . I might get some understanding of why. . . . Why my life has grown so empty and meaningless. Why I've turned into a hateful, quarrelsome, old woman. And before I leave this earth, I'd like to recover some of the dignity . . . the peace I used to know. For I'm going to die . . . and Jessie Mae knows that . . . and she's willful and it's her will I die in those two rooms. Well, she won't have her way. It's my will to die in Bountiful. (*She sobs and starts to run out of the Bus Station. The Sheriff stops her. She suddenly seems very weak, and is about to fall. He has her arm, supporting her.*)

SHERIFF. Mrs. Watts.

MRS. WATTS. Let me go those twelve miles . . . before it's too late. (*A pause. For a moment her strength seems to come back.*) Understand me. Suffering I don't mind. Suffering I understand. I never protested once. Though my heart was broken when those babies died. I could stand seeing the man I love walk through life with another woman. But this fifteen years of bickering. Endless, petty bickering. . . . It's made me like Jessie Mae sees me. It's ugly. I won't be that way. (*An anguished cry.*) I want to go home. I want to go home. I want to go . . . (*She is unable to speak any more. She is on the verge of collapse. The Sheriff helps her over to the bench and settles her there. The Sheriff calls to the Ticket Man.*)

SHERIFF. Roy, hurry. Call a doctor. (*She summons up her last bit of strength to get free.*)

MRS. WATTS. No. No doctor. Bountiful. . . . Bountiful. . . . Bountiful. (*The Sheriff holds her. There is a very fast curtain.*)

## END OF ACT TWO

# ACT III

SCENE: *It is early morning. The lights are slowly brought up and we can see the house and the yard of Mrs. Watts' old house in Bountiful. The house, with a sagging porch before it, is* R. *The entrance to the yard is* U. C.
*The house is an old ramshackle, two story country place that hasn't been painted for years. Vines are growing wild over it, coral vine and Virginia Creeper and fig vine. The roof of the front porch is sagging and one of the supporting posts is completely gone. The floor boards of the front porch are rotting away and the steps leading to the porch are loose. The yard has gone to weeds and wild flowers are everywhere: Buttercups, dandelions and wild iris. In the early morning light there is a peace and tranquillity and a wild kind of beauty about the place that is moving and heart warming and in its own way lovely. The Sheriff and Mrs. Watts come in* U. C. *walking very slowly. They stop every few minutes while she looks at the house and the yard. Mrs. Watts is carrying her purse.*

MRS. WATTS. I'm home. I'm home. I'm home. Thank you. I thank you. I thank you. I thank you. (*They pause for a moment in the yard. Mrs. Watts is obviously still quite weak.*)
SHERIFF. You'd better sit down and rest for a while. You don't want to overdo it.
MRS. WATTS. Yessir. (*She sits on a tree stump in the yard.*)
SHERIFF. Feeling all right?
MRS. WATTS. Yes, I am. I feel ever so much better.
SHERIFF. You look better. I hope I've done the right thing in bringing you here. Well, I don't see what harm it can do. As long as you mind the doctor and don't get over excited.
MRS. WATTS. Yessir. (*A pause. She looks around the yard again.*)
SHERIFF. Soon as you've rested for a little I'll go on back to my

57

car and leave you alone. You can call me if you need anything.
I'll stay out here until your son arrives.

MRS. WATTS. Thank you. You've been very kind. (*A bird calls. She and the Sheriff sit listening to it. It whistles once again.*) What kind of a bird was that?

SHERIFF. Red bird.

MRS. WATTS. I thought that was a red bird, but I hadn't heard one in so long, I couldn't be sure. (*A pause.*) Do they still have scissor tails around here?

SHERIFF. Yes, Ma'm. I still see one every once in a while when I'm driving around the country.

MRS. WATTS. I don't know of anything prettier than a scissor tail flying around in the sky. (*A pause.*) My father was a good man in many ways, a peculiar man, but a good one. One of the things he couldn't stand was to see a bird shot on his land. If men came here hunting, he'd take a gun and chase them away. I think the birds knew they couldn't be touched here. Our land was always a home to them. Ducks and geese and finches and blue jays. Blue birds and red birds. Wild canaries and black birds and mockers and doves and rice birds . . . (*During the latter speech she gets up and begins to pick weeds out of the yard. At the end of the speech the Sheriff gently stops her and leads her to the porch of the house. She sits on step.*)

SHERIFF. Rice birds are gettin' thicker every year. They seem to thrive out here on the coast.

MRS. WATTS. I guess a mockin' bird is my favorite of them all.

SHERIFF. I guess it's mine, too.

MRS. WATTS. I don't know, though. I'm mighty partial to a scissor tail. I hope I get to see one soon.

SHERIFF. I hope you can.

MRS. WATTS. My father was born on this land and in this house. Did you know my father?

SHERIFF. No, Ma'm. Not that I can remember.

MRS. WATTS. I guess there are not many around here that remember my father. I do, of course, and my son. Maybe some old timers around Harrison. (*A pause.*) It's funny, ever since I've been here I've been half expectin' my father and my mother to walk out of the house and greet me and welcome me home. (*A pause.*) When you've lived longer than your house or your family, maybe you've lived too long. (*A pause.*) Or maybe it's just me.

58

Maybe the need to belong to a house, and a family and a town has gone from the rest of the world.

SHERIFF. How big was your farm, Mrs. Watts?

MRS. WATTS. Three hundred and seventy-five acres were left when my papa died and I sold off all but the house and the yard. (*A pause.*) You say the store burned fifteen years ago?

SHERIFF. Yes, Ma'm. What was left of it. You see with the good roads we have now in the county, the little town and their country stores are all disappearing. The farmers ride into Cotton or Harrison to trade. . . .

MRS. WATTS. But what's happened to the farms? For the last five miles I've seen nothing but woods. . . .

SHERIFF. I know. The land around Bountiful just played out. People like you got discouraged and moved away, sold off the land for what they could get. H. T. Mavis bought most of it up. He let it go back into timber. He keeps a few head of cattle out here. That's about all. . . .

MRS. WATTS. Callie Davis kept her farm going.

SHERIFF. Yes. She did. She learned how to treat her land right and it began paying off for her toward the end. I've heard she was out riding her tractor the day before she died. Lonely death she had. All by herself in that big house.

MRS. WATTS. There are worse things. (*The sun is up full now. Filling the stage with light.*)

SHERIFF. Looks to me like you're going to have a pretty day.

MRS. WATTS. I hope so. My daughter-in-law has never seen our place in the sunshine. I expect my son will bring her along with him. I'd hate for her to have to see it again in the rain. (*A pause. The Sheriff looks at her.*)

SHERIFF. Feeling more rested now?

MRS. WATTS. Oh, yes, I am.

SHERIFF. Good. Then I'll be getting on back to my car. You just call me if you need anything.

MRS. WATTS. Thank you. (*He gets up and walks to the corner of the yard. Just before he goes out he turns and waves. Mrs. Watts waves back to him. She sits on the steps for a moment watching him go out u. c. When he is out of sight, she rises slowly from the steps and goes along the porch. When she comes to the front door she stops and stands for a moment. She slowly opens the door and goes inside the house as the lights fade. The lights*)

*are slowly brought up. The Sheriff comes into the yard. He goes up to the steps of the porch.)*
SHERIFF. *(Calling.)* Mrs. Watts. Mrs. Watts. Mrs. Watts. *(He runs up on the porch as he calls her. Mrs. Watts comes out of the house. She has left her purse inside the house.)*
MRS. WATTS. Yessir.
SHERIFF. It's seven-thirty. Your son and his wife are here.
MRS. WATTS. Yessir.
SHERIFF. They're out on the road in their car. They said they had to hurry on back. I told them I'd come get you.
MRS. WATTS. Yessir. Won't you ask them to please come in for a minute?
SHERIFF. Well, all right. I'll have to be gettin' on back to town now myself, Mrs. Watts. *(He holds his hand out. She takes it.)* Goodbye, and good luck to you.
MRS. WATTS. Thank you. You'll never know what this has meant to me.
SHERIFF. Glad I could oblige. *(He starts away as Ludie comes into the yard* U. C.*)* Oh, Mr. Watts. I was just coming to tell you your mother wanted you to come in for a few minutes.
LUDIE. Thank you. *(The Sheriff goes up to him.)*
SHERIFF. I've got to be getting back on into town.
LUDIE. All right, Sheriff. Thank you for everything you've done.
SHERIFF. Don't mention it. I was glad I could oblige. You folks have a nice trip home.
LUDIE. Thank you.
SHERIFF. Goodbye, Mrs. Watts.
MRS. WATTS. Goodbye, Sheriff.
SHERIFF. So long, Mr. Watts.
LUDIE. Goodbye, Sheriff. *(He goes out* U. C. *Mrs. Watts and Ludie watch him go. Ludie walks up on the porch to his mother. They both seem embarrassed and ill at ease.)* Hello, Mama.
MRS. WATTS. Hello, son.
LUDIE. How do you feel?
MRS. WATTS. I'm feelin' better, Ludie.
LUDIE. That's good. They told me at the bus station you had another attack.
MRS. WATTS. Yes, I did. All the excitement, I guess. But I feel fine now.
LUDIE. Yes'm.

MRS. WATTS. I got my wish.
LUDIE. Yes'm. (*Ludie walks away from the porch down to the corner of the yard. Mrs. Watts follows him.*)
MRS. WATTS. I hope I didn't worry you too much, Ludie. But I just felt I had to . . .
LUDIE. I know, Mama.
MRS. WATTS. You see, son, I know it's hard for you to understand and Jessie Mae . . . understand—But . . .
LUDIE. Yes, Ma'm. I understand, Mama. It's done now. So let's forget about it.
MRS. WATTS. All right, sonny. (*A pause.*) You did bring Jessie Mae, didn't you?
LUDIE. Yes, Ma'm.
MRS. WATTS. Well, now she's here isn't she going to get out of the car and look around a little?
LUDIE. She didn't seem to want to, Mama.
MRS. WATTS. You asked her?
LUDIE. Yes, Ma'm. (*A pause.*)
MRS. WATTS. Did you ask about your raise, son?
LUDIE. Yes, Ma'm, and Mr. Douglas told me he liked my work and he'd be glad to recommend a raise for me.
MRS. WATTS. Oh. (*A pause.*) The sky's so blue, Ludie. Did you ever see the sky so blue?
LUDIE. No, Ma'm. (*A pause.*)
MRS. WATTS. Callie Davis died.
LUDIE. Is that so? When did that happen?
MRS. WATTS. They don't rightly know. They found her dead. She'd been ridin' a tractor the day before they found her. Buried her yesterday. (*A pause.*)
LUDIE. Mama, I should have made myself bring you here before. I'm sorry but I thought it would be easier for both of us not to see the house again.
MRS. WATTS. I know, Ludie. (*A pause.*) Now you're here, wouldn't you like to come inside, son, and look around?
LUDIE. I don't think I'd better, Mama. I don't see any use in it. It would just make me feel bad. I'd rather remember it like it was. (*A pause. Mrs. Watts looks at the house. She smiles.*)
MRS. WATTS. The old house has gotten kind of run down, hasn't it?
LUDIE. Yes, it has. (*She starts back toward the house slowly.*)

MRS. WATTS. I don't think it'll last out the next Gulf storm.

LUDIE. It doesn't look like it would. (*She turns and looks at him standing in the yard.*)

MRS. WATTS. You know who you look like standing there, Ludie?

LUDIE. Who?

MRS. WATTS. My Papa.

LUDIE. Do I?

MRS. WATTS. Just like him. Of course, I've been noticing as you grow older you look more and more like him. My Papa was a good-looking man.

LUDIE. Was he?

MRS. WATTS. You've seen his pictures. Didn't you think so?

LUDIE. I don't remember. It's been so long since I looked at his picture.

MRS. WATTS. Well, he was always considered a very nice looking man. (*A pause.*) Do you remember my Papa at all, son? (*Mrs. Watts sits on the steps of the porch.*)

LUDIE. No, Ma'm. Not too well. I was only ten when he died, Mama. I remember the day he died. I heard about it as I was coming home from school. Lee Weems told me. I thought he was joking and I called him a liar. I remember you takin' me into the front room there the day of the funeral to say goodbye to him. I remember the coffin and the people sitting in the room. Old man Joe Weems took me up on his knee and told me that Grandpapa was his best friend and that his life was a real example for me to follow. I remember Grandmama sitting by the coffin crying and she made me promise that when I had a son of my own I'd name it after Grandpapa. I would have, too. I've never forgotten that promise. (*A pause.*) Well, I didn't have a son. Or a daughter. (*A pause.*) Billy Davidson told me his wife is expecting her fourth child. They have two girls and a boy, now. Billy Davidson doesn't make much more than I do and they certainly seem to get along. Own their own home and have a car. It does your heart good to hear them tell about how they all get along. Everybody has their job, even the youngest child. She's only three. She puts the napkins around the table at meal times. That's her job. Billy said to me, Ludie, I don't know how I'd keep going without my kids. He said I don't understand what keeps you going, Ludie. What you work for. I said, Well, Billy . . . Oh, Mama, I haven't made any kind of life for you, either one of you and I try so hard. I try so hard. (*He crosses to her.*) Oh, Mama. I lied to you. I do remember. I remember so much. This house. The life here. The night you woke me up and dressed me and took me for a walk when there was a full moon and I cried because I was afraid and you comforted me. (*He turns abruptly away from his mother and walks to the down stage corner of the porch.*) Mama, I want to stop remembering. . . . It doesn't do any good to remember. (*A car horn is heard in the distance. Loud and impatient. He looks in the direction of the horn.*) That's Jessie Mae.

MRS. WATTS. Whose car did you come in? (*He crosses to her.*)

LUDIE. I borrowed Billy Davidson's car. He didn't want me to have it at first. You know people are funny about lending their car, but then I explained what happened and he was nice about it. (*The car horn is heard again.*) We have to start back now, Mama. Jessie Mae is nervous that I might lose my job.

MRS. WATTS. (*Frantically trying to find an excuse not to leave.*) Didn't you ask for the day off?

LUDIE. No, Ma'm. I only asked for the morning off.

MRS. WATTS. What time is it now?

LUDIE. Must be after eight. We were a little late getting here.

MRS. WATTS. We can drive it in three hours, can't we, Ludie?

LUDIE. Yes, Ma'm, but we might have a flat or run into traffic or something. Besides, I promised Billy I'd get his car back to him by twelve.

MRS. WATTS. Son, why am I going back at all? Why can't I stay?

LUDIE. Mama, you can't stay. You know that. Now come on. (*He takes her by the arm. She starts to get up from the steps. When she is about half way up she collapses crying. She cries passionately, openly, bitterly.*)

MRS. WATTS. Ludie. Ludie. What's happened to us? Why have we come to this?

LUDIE. I don't know, Mama.

MRS. WATTS. To have stayed and fought the land would have been better than this.

LUDIE. Yes'm. (*She gets up.*)

MRS. WATTS. Pretty soon it'll all be gone. Ten years . . . twenty . . . this house . . . me . . . you. . . .

LUDIE. I know, Mama. (*A pause. She looks in his suffering face. She looks around. She speaks with great tenderness.*)
MRS. WATTS. But the river will be here. The fields. The woods. The smell of the Gulf. That's what I always took my strength from, Ludie. Not from houses, not from people. (*A pause.*) It's so quiet. It's so eternally quiet. I had forgotten the peace. The quiet. And it's given me strength once more, Ludie. To go on and do what I have to do. I've found my dignity and my strength.
LUDIE. I'm glad, Mama.
MRS. WATTS. And I'll never fight with Jessie Mae again or complain. (*She points out into the distance.*) Do you remember how my Papa always had that field over there planted in cotton?
LUDIE. Yes, Ma'm.
MRS. WATTS. See, it's all woods now. But I expect some day people will come again and cut down the trees and plant the cotton and maybe even wear out the land again and then their children will sell it and go to the cities and then the trees will come up again.
LUDIE. I expect so, Mama.
MRS. WATTS. We're part of all this. We left it, but we can never lose what it has given us.
LUDIE. I expect so, Mama. (*He takes her by the arm and they start walking out. Jessie Mae comes into the yard u. c.*)
JESSIE MAE. Ludie. Are you coming or not?
LUDIE. We were just startin', Jessie Mae.
MRS. WATTS. Hello, Jessie Mae.
JESSIE MAE. I'm not speakin' to you. I guess you're proud of the time you gave us. Dragging us all the way out here this time of the mornin'. If Ludie loses his job over this, I hope you're satisfied.
LUDIE. I'm not goin' to lose my job, Jessie Mae.
JESSIE MAE. Well, you could.
LUDIE. All right, Jessie Mae.
JESSIE MAE. And she should realize that. She's selfish. That's her trouble. Always has been. Just purdee selfish. Did you tell your Mama what we were discussing in the car?
LUDIE. No. We can talk it all over driving back to Houston.
JESSIE MAE. I think we should have it all out right here. I'd like everything understood right now. (*Jessie Mae opens her purse and takes out a piece of paper.*) I've gotten everything written down.

Do you want to read it or do you want me to read it to you, Mother Watts?

MRS. WATTS. What is it, Jessie Mae?

JESSIE MAE. It's a few rules and regulations that are necessary to my peace of mind. And I think to Ludie's. Ludie says you may have a few of your own to add and that may be and I'm perfectly willin' to listen if you do. . . . First of all, I'd like to ask you a question.

MRS. WATTS. Yes, Ma'm. (*Mrs. Watts sits on the steps.*)

JESSIE MAE. Just what possessed you to run away? Didn't you know you'd be caught and have to come back?

MRS. WATTS. I had to come, Jessie Mae. Twenty years is a long time.

JESSIE MAE. But what if you had died from the excitement! Didn't you know you could have died?

MRS. WATTS. I knew.

JESSIE MAE. And you didn't care?

MRS. WATTS. (*With great dignity.*) I had to come, Jessie Mae.

JESSIE MAE. Well, I hope it's out of your system now.

MRS. WATTS. It is. I've had my trip. That's more than enough to keep me happy the rest of my life.

JESSIE MAE. Well, I'm glad to hear it. That's the first thing on my list. (*She reads from list.*) Number one. There'll be no more running away.

MRS. WATTS. There'll be no more running away.

JESSIE MAE. Good. (*She takes the list up again.*) Number two. No more hymn singing, when I'm in the apartment. When I'm gone you can sing your lungs out. Agreed?

MRS. WATTS. Agreed.

JESSIE MAE. Number three.

LUDIE. (*Interrupting.*) Jessie Mae, can't this wait till we get home?

JESSIE MAE. Now, honey, we agreed that I'm going to handle this! (*She goes back to list.*) No more pouting. When I ask a question, I'd like an answer. Otherwise I'll consider it's pouting.

MRS. WATTS. All right.

JESSIE MAE. Fourth. With the condition that your heart is in I feel you should not run around the apartment when you can walk.

MRS. WATTS. All right, Jessie Mae.

JESSIE MAE. That's all. Is there anything you want to say to me?

MRS. WATTS. No, Jessie Mae.

JESSIE MAE. I might as well tell you now I'm not staying in the house and watching over you any more. I am joinin' a bridge club and going to town at least twice a week. If you go now, it'll just be your funeral. You understand?

MRS. WATTS. I understand.

JESSIE MAE. All right. (*She puts the list away.*)

LUDIE. And, Mama, we also agreed that we're all gonna try our best to get along together. Jessie Mae also realizes that she gets upset sometimes when she shouldn't. Don't you, Jessie Mae?

JESSIE MAE. Uh huh.

LUDIE. So let's start by trying to have a pleasant ride home.

JESSIE MAE. Allrightie. (*She takes a cigarette and the lighter from her purse. The lighter works and she lights her cigarette. She crosses down to the far edge of the house.*) Is there any water around here? I'm thirsty.

LUDIE. I don't think so, Jessie Mae. Mama, is there any water around here?

MRS. WATTS. No. The cistern is gone. (*Jessie Mae notices a scratch on her shoes. She is furious.*)

JESSIE MAE. Look at my shoes! I've got scratches on them. They're my good pair. I ought to have my head examined for wearing my only good pair of shoes out here in this old swamp.

LUDIE. (*Looking out in the distance.*) When I was a boy I used to drink in the creek over there, Jessie Mae. We had a cistern, but I always preferred to drink out of the creek. It seemed to me the water always tasted so much better. (*Jessie Mae crosses over to the far end of the stage looking out at the creek in the distance.*)

JESSIE MAE. Well, you wouldn't catch me drinking out of any creek. I knew a man once that went on a huntin' trip and drank out of a creek and caught something and died.

MRS. WATTS. There's nothin' like cistern water for washin' your hair with. It is the softest water in the world. (*A bird calls in the distance.*) That's a red bird.

JESSIE MAE. A what?

MRS. WATTS. A red bird.

JESSIE MAE. Oh. I thought you said that. They all sound alike

66

to me. Well, come on. Let's get going. Do we go back by the way of Harrison?

LUDIE. Yes.

JESSIE MAE. Good. Then we can stop at the drug store. I'm so thirsty I could drink ten Coca-colas. Are you all ready?

MRS. WATTS. Yes'm. (*They start out. Jessie Mae looks at her.*)

JESSIE MAE. Where's your purse?

MRS. WATTS. Are you talkin' to me, Jessie Mae?

JESSIE MAE. Who else would I be talkin' to? Since when did Ludie start walkin' around with a pocket book under his arm? (*Mrs. Watts looks around.*)

MRS. WATTS. Oh, I guess I left it inside.

JESSIE MAE. Where? (*She starts toward the door of the house.*)

MRS. WATTS. I'll get it. (*She turns to go into the house.*)

JESSIE MAE. No. I want to go. You'll take all day. Where did you leave it?

MRS. WATTS. In the parlour. Right off the front hall.

JESSIE MAE. All right. I'll get it. You wait here. (*She starts in the house. She turns and sees them walking off* U. C.) I said wait here now. I don't want to be left alone in this ramshackly old house. No telling what's running around in there.

MRS. WATTS. There's nothing in there.

JESSIE MAE. There might be rats or snakes or something.

LUDIE. I'll go.

JESSIE MAE. No. I'll go. Just stay here so if I holler you can come. (*She goes inside the house. Ludie turns to his mother.*)

LUDIE. Mama.

MRS. WATTS. It's all right, Ludie, son. (*Jessie Mae comes back out with the purse.*)

JESSIE MAE. Here's your purse. Now where's the money for that Government check?

MRS. WATTS. I haven't cashed it.

JESSIE MAE. Where is it?

MRS. WATTS. It's right inside the purse. (*Jessie Mae opens the purse and begins to search again.*)

JESSIE MAE. No. It isn't.

MRS. WATTS. Here. Let me look. (*Jessie Mae hands her the purse and Mrs. Watts, too, begins to rummage around. All of a sudden she bursts out laughing.*)

67

JESSIE MAE. What's the matter with you?

MRS. WATTS. That's a good joke on me.

JESSIE MAE. Well, what's so funny?

MRS. WATTS. I just remembered. I left this purse on the bus last night and caused a man a lot of trouble because I thought the check was in there. (*She is overcome by laughter again.*) And do you know that check wasn't in that purse all that time?

JESSIE MAE. Where was it?

MRS. WATTS. Right here. (*She reaches inside her dress and takes it out.*) Been here since yesterday afternoon. (*Jessie Mae reaches for the check.*)

JESSIE MAE. Give it to me before you go and lose it again.

MRS. WATTS. I won't lose it.

JESSIE MAE. Now don't start that business again. Just give it to me.

LUDIE. (*Interrupting angrily.*) Jessie Mae.

JESSIE MAE. Well, I'm not going to——

LUDIE. (*With great positiveness*). We're going to stop this wrangling once and for all. You've given me your word and I expect you to keep your word. We have to live together and we're going to live together in peace.

MRS. WATTS. It's all right, Ludie. (*She gives the check to Jessie Mae.*) Let Jessie Mae take care of the check. (*Jessie Mae accepts the check. She looks at it for a moment and then grabs Mrs. Watts' purse. She opens it and puts the check inside.*)

JESSIE MAE. Oh, here. You keep the check. But don't go and lose it before you get home. (*She puts the purse back in Mrs. Watts' hand. She starts off stage* u. c.) Well, come on. Let's go. (*She leaves. Ludie goes to his mother.*)

LUDIE. Mama, if I get the raise you won't——

MRS. WATTS. It's all right, Ludie. I've had my trip. You go ahead. I'll be right there. (*Ludie starts out* u. c. *Mrs. Watts points up in the sky.*) Look, isn't that a scissor tail?

LUDIE. I don't know. I didn't get to see it if it was. They fly so fast. (*Ludie takes one last look at the house.*) The house used to look so big. (*He goes out. Mrs. Watts stands for a moment looking into the sky. Then she drops gently on her knees, puts her hands in the dirt. She kneels for a moment holding the dirt, then slowly lets it drift through her fingers back to the ground. She*

*begins to walk slowly out* U. C. *until she gets to the corner of the yard. She pauses for a moment, taking one last look at the house, speaks quietly.)*
MRS. WATTS. Goodbye, Bountiful, goodbye. *(Then she turns and walks off the stage* U. C.*)*

## CURTAIN

## PROPERTY PLOT

### ACT I, Scene 1

Movie magazine on desk in living room
Book on living room table
Cigarettes and lighter (doesn't work) in Jessie Mae's dressing gown pocket
Matches in pocket of Ludie's dressing gown
Glass of milk—offstage for Mrs. Watts
Recipe in drawer of vanity in bedroom
Pension check for Mrs. Watts—under D. R. corner of living room rug
Cigarettes, ash tray, hair curlers, hair net, face cream, hair brush, etc. on vanity in bedroom
Clothing in wardrobe in living room

### ACT I, Scene 2

Newspaper on desk in living room
Dress for Jessie Mae in bedroom closet
Check for Mrs. Watts
Breakfast tray and dishes—Mrs. Watts
Tape measure in wardrobe in living room
Carpet sweeper and dust rag—offstage for Mrs. Watts
Glass of water—offstage for Jessie Mae
Writing paper and envelope in desk in living room
Hat and purse—Jessie Mae, in bedroom
Hat, purse, coat—Mrs. Watts, in wardrobe in living room

### ACT II

Bus tickets
Suitcase—Mrs. Watts
Hat, coat, purse with handkerchief in it—Mrs. Watts

69

Suitcase and in it a sandwich wrapped in paper—Thelma
Magazine—Thelma
Hat and purse with comb, make-up, cigarettes and lighter (doesn't
    work) in it—Jessie Mae
Matches—Thelma, in jacket pocket
Movie magazine—offstage for Ludie
Handkerchief—Ludie's pocket
Pile of newspapers—offstage for Harrison Ticket Man
Crate—offstage for Harrison Ticket Man

## Act III

Purse—Mrs. Watts
Purse with paper, cigarettes and lighter (works this time) in it—Jessie
    Mae

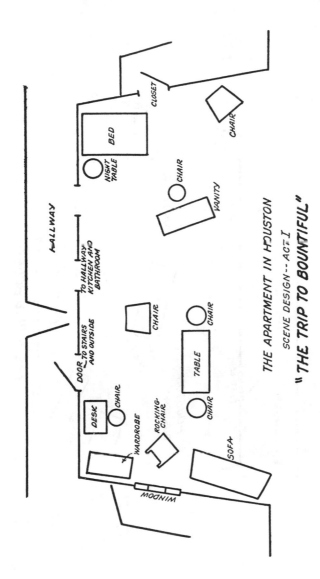

HALLWAY

CLOSET

BED

NIGHT TABLE

CHAIR

CHAIR

VANITY

TO HALLWAY KITCHEN AND BATHROOM

DOOR TO STAIRS AND OUTSIDE

CHAIR

CHAIR

TABLE

CHAIR

DESK

CHAIR

WARDROBE

ROCKING-CHAIR

SOFA

WINDOW

THE APARTMENT IN HOUSTON

SCENE DESIGN--ACT I

"THE TRIP TO BOUNTIFUL"

71

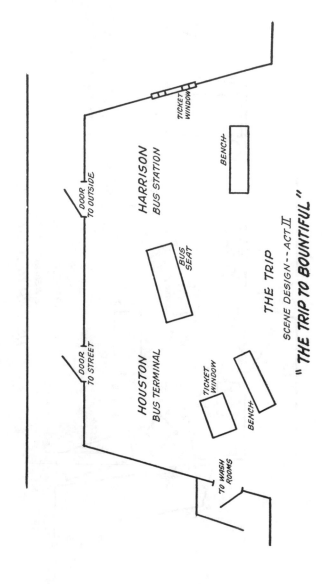

THE TRIP
SCENE DESIGN--ACT II

"THE TRIP TO BOUNTIFUL"

# NEW
# PLAYS

## THE AFRICAN COMPANY PRESENTS
## RICHARD III
### by Carlyle Brown

## EDWARD ALBEE'S
## FRAGMENTS and THE MARRIAGE PLAY

## IMAGINARY LIFE
### by Peter Parnell

## MIXED EMOTIONS
### by Richard Baer

## THE SWAN
### by Elizabeth Egloff

*Write for information as to
availability*
**DRAMATISTS PLAY SERVICE, Inc.**
440 Park Avenue South    New York, N.Y. 10016

# NEW
# PLAYS

### THE LIGHTS
by Howard Korder

### THE TRIUMPH OF LOVE
by James Magruder

### LATER LIFE
by A.R. Gurney

### THE LOMAN FAMILY PICNIC
by Donald Margulies

### A PERFECT GANESH
by Terrence McNally

### SPAIN
by Romulus Linney

*Write for information as to availability*
**DRAMATISTS PLAY SERVICE, Inc.**
440 Park Avenue South      New York, N.Y. 10016

# NEW
# PLAYS

### LONELY PLANET
by Steven Dietz

### THE AMERICA PLAY
by Suzan-Lori Parks

### THE FOURTH WALL
by A.R. Gurney

### JULIE JOHNSON
by Wendy Hammond

### FOUR DOGS AND A BONE
by John Patrick Shanley

### DESDEMONA, A PLAY ABOUT A
### HANDKERCHIEF
by Paula Vogel

*Write for information as to*
*availability*
**DRAMATISTS PLAY SERVICE, Inc.**
440 Park Avenue South      New York, N.Y. 10016